Invest With A SMILE

By

George C. Knowlton III

ISBN: 979-8-9924778-1-8

Dedication

This book is dedicated to the men and women of America and around the world. The strength of what was once known as the "middle class" lies in financial education and a shared commitment to community well-being. By empowering individuals with knowledge, we can preserve and uplift a way of life built on opportunity, stability, and growth.

For the novice investor, this book serves as a step-by-step guide to real estate investing—offering a clear framework to assess opportunities and evaluate investment operators with confidence.

For the seasoned investor, this book provides a wealth of insights into the latest AI-driven strategies, equipping you with the tools to elevate your success and stay ahead in an ever-evolving market.

May these pages inspire action, informed decision-making, and a future of financial empowerment for all.

Acknowledgements

First and foremost, I give thanks to God for thinking of me. Without the relationship we share, this book would not have come to life.

To the many mentors mentioned in these pages, I extend my deepest gratitude. Some of you guided me knowingly, while others influenced me through your actions, perspectives, successes, and even failures—many of which I had the privilege to witness. A few of you took the time to teach me what I didn't yet realize I needed to learn.

Together, you have woven the fabric that holds this book together. It is my sincere hope that these words honor your achievements, celebrate your strengths, and shine a light on your contributions in a way that fills you with pride.

Table of Contents

Chapter 1
Navigating the Real Estate Landscape with SMILE

Introduction to SMILE Philosophy

In the rapidly evolving world of real estate, success demands a multifaceted approach that transcends traditional profit-centric strategies. SMILE Company LLC has championed a philosophy that incorporates ethical, social, and financial elements to foster balanced growth. SMILE—an acronym for Safety, Morality, Inclusivity, Linguistic Clarity, and Experiential Learning—serves as a guiding framework for modern investors.

The groundbreaking tenets of SMILE are built on the recognition that real estate investments impact not just portfolios, but also communities and environments. By prioritizing sustainability and ethical considerations, SMILE provides a roadmap for investors seeking both financial returns and positive societal impact.

Renowned real estate investor Barbara Corcoran, known for founding The Corcoran Group and appearing on Shark Tank, has often emphasized the importance of balancing profitability with ethics. Corcoran frequently shares her experiences of transforming neglected properties into thriving community hubs, demonstrating how socially responsible investing can lead to significant financial success. One notable project involved a distressed building in New York City that, after renovation and community engagement, saw property values increase by over 40% within three years.

This chapter explores the foundational principles of SMILE and how investors can apply these principles to navigate the complexities of modern real estate markets while creating lasting value.

Understanding the Market Dynamics

Trends Shaping the Industry

The real estate market is a dynamic and complex entity, influenced by a myriad of factors including economic trends, societal shifts, and technological advancements. Over recent years, significant changes have emerged, reshaping the investment landscape. Understanding these trends is essential for investors to make informed decisions.

Mark Zandi, Chief Economist at Moody's Analytics, highlights that the shift to remote work has permanently altered housing markets. One study he referenced showed a 25% increase in suburban housing demand in key markets like Phoenix and Atlanta. This trend underscores the importance of understanding regional demographic shifts when making investment decisions.

Economic Trends

Interest rates, inflation, and governmental fiscal policies play a crucial role in determining real estate value and investment viability. Historically, lower interest rates have spurred property purchases, while inflation concerns can increase the attractiveness of real assets as a hedge. For example, during periods of high inflation, investors often turn to real estate as a stable, tangible asset that can preserve wealth.

Recent developments highlight that mortgage rates have begun to decrease following recent Federal Reserve interest rate cuts, offering potential relief to homebuyers. However, the housing supply remains tight due to high building costs and regulatory delays, posing ongoing affordability challenges for buyers.

Certain regions are emerging as hotspots for real estate investment. Cities like Buffalo, Indianapolis, and Providence are experiencing strong demand coupled with limited housing supply, leading to increased competition among buyers and a rise in home values. For instance, Buffalo has been named the hottest housing market for 2025, with home values expected to rise by another 3% this year following a 6% increase in 2024.

Societal Shifts

Demographic changes, including aging populations and shifting work habits, are pivotal. The COVID-19 pandemic accelerated a move towards remote work, prompting a migration from dense urban centers to more spacious suburban locales. This shift has significantly impacted housing demand and investment opportunities. Understanding these shifts allows investors to target emerging markets and adapt to changing consumer preferences.

A noteworthy demographic trend is the rising influence of affluent women in the luxury real estate market. Women with significant wealth are increasingly involved in buying and selling luxury homes, as well as making key decisions in home design. This shift reflects broader trends of women taking greater control over their finances and investments.

Sustainability and Technological Integration

There is a growing emphasis on sustainability and the integration of technology in real estate. Investors are increasingly focusing on eco-friendly properties and smart home technologies to meet the evolving preferences of consumers and to comply with environmental regulations. This trend is expected to enhance property values and attract environmentally conscious buyers.

Additionally, the rise of AI-driven property analyses is empowering investors with precise market insights, reducing risks, and enabling faster decision-making. This trend underscores the importance of integrating technological advancements with ethical considerations to optimize investment outcomes.

By closely monitoring these trends—including mortgage rates, regional market dynamics, sustainability initiatives, demographic shifts, and technological advancements—investors can better navigate the evolving real estate landscape in 2025 and beyond.

The Urban to Suburban Shift

The migration trend towards suburbs has reshaped investment strategies, bringing new opportunities and challenges. Historically linked to factors like affordability and quality of life, this transition has only intensified post-pandemic. Recent reports indicate that suburban and exurban areas, previously overlooked, are now seeing significant growth due to their affordability and spacious living options.

Historical Context

Previous migration waves, spurred by industrialization and urban sprawl, set the foundation for current trends. During the mid-20th century, suburban development boomed as families sought more space and better living conditions outside crowded cities. Today, similar factors are driving a renewed interest in suburban areas, but with additional considerations such as remote work capabilities and community-focused living.

Real estate mogul Sam Zell, known for his expertise in multifamily and commercial real estate, has discussed the cyclical nature of urban-to-suburban shifts. In the early 1990s, during a recession, Zell adopted a contrarian investment approach by focusing on high-quality urban assets through Equity Office Properties (EOP), while most investors shifted their focus to suburban office properties. By 1996, Zell had built up an office portfolio valued at $4.8 billion, consisting of 32 million square feet in 90 buildings. His strategy showcased the importance of timing and understanding demographic shifts to capitalize on market trends.

Current Trends

The pandemic accelerated the move from crowded cities to spacious suburbs. This migration reshaped the demand for multifamily housing in suburban areas, providing investors with new opportunities. According to recent studies, suburban properties have seen a significant increase in demand, particularly those that offer amenities like green spaces, home offices, and proximity to essential services.

Recent reports highlight those exurban areas—those located beyond traditional suburbs—are witnessing significant population growth. For instance, Haines City in Polk County, Florida, saw an influx of nearly 30,000 new residents last year, making it the top destination for new moves in the U.S. Similarly, cities like Anna, Texas, have experienced rapid growth due to rising housing costs in closer suburban areas and a desire for more spacious living environments.

Recent reports indicate also that suburban areas labeled as "hidden gem" cities, such as those highlighted by Opendoor's 2024 housing report, have emerged as hotspots for property investment. These regions offer more affordable housing options while maintaining access to urban amenities. For instance, cities like Charlotte, North Carolina, and Boise, Idaho, have seen significant growth due to their balance of affordability and quality of life.

Understanding these shifts allows investors to target emerging markets and adapt to changing consumer preferences, ensuring their investments remain impactful and profitable for years to come.

The Atlantic's recent analysis further explores the demographic shift, noting that urban families are increasingly seeking suburban or exurban lifestyles. This shift is driven by factors such as better schools, safety, and community-focused living environments. The article highlights that cities like Austin and Nashville are prime examples of how suburban areas are adapting to these new demands by offering mixed-use developments that cater to modern living preferences.

Case studies from regions like Denver, Colorado, and Charlotte, North Carolina, illustrate how suburban investments have surged in popularity. One mixed-use development in Denver transformed a vacant shopping mall into a vibrant community with residential units, retail spaces, and public parks, achieving a 98% occupancy rate within its first year.

The migration trend towards suburbs has reshaped investment strategies, bringing new opportunities and challenges. Historically linked to factors like affordability and quality of life, this transition has only intensified post-pandemic.

Sustainability as a Market Driver

Sustainability has emerged as a pivotal force in real estate development. As environmental consciousness rises, sustainable practices become not only desirable but necessary. Green buildings and energy-efficient systems lead the charge, supported by governmental policies and incentives promoting low-carbon footprints.

Balancing profitability with sustainability is no longer an option but a necessity. Developers incorporating green spaces, renewable energy solutions, and sustainable materials are seeing higher property values and increased tenant satisfaction. A recent development in Seattle, for instance, featured solar-powered public spaces and energy-efficient appliances, reducing utility costs by 30% and increasing tenant retention rates.

As sustainability continues to drive market demand, investors who prioritize green properties are positioning themselves for long-term success. By embracing these trends, investors and developers can create more value-driven and socially responsible real estate solutions, ensuring their investments remain impactful and profitable for years to come.

Environmental Impact

The real estate industry is undergoing significant transformations, with sustainability and technological advancements at the forefront of this evolution. Investors and developers are increasingly recognizing the value of integrating eco-friendly practices and cutting-edge technologies to meet the demands of modern consumers and regulatory standards.

Green certifications, such as LEED (Leadership in Energy and Environmental Design), are now key factors influencing property value. These certifications signify a property's commitment to environmental sustainability, which can lead to higher property values and increased demand from eco-conscious buyers and tenants. For instance, a study highlighted by Uhoo demonstrates how buildings with green certifications achieve higher rental rates and attract long-term tenants.

In 2025, Environmental, Social, and Governance (ESG) considerations continue to evolve as pivotal drivers in real estate development and asset management. As regulatory frameworks tighten, investor expectations rise, and tenants demand more sustainable and equitable spaces, real estate professionals must stay ahead of the curve. This shift is particularly noticeable in urban redevelopment projects where sustainability and community engagement are prioritized.

Technological Innovations in Real Estate

The adoption of PropTech solutions, such as solar energy systems, water conservation technologies, and sustainable building materials, is further contributing to eco-friendly real estate solutions. For example, the Edge building in Amsterdam, often referred to as the world's smartest building, uses IoT to optimize energy consumption and enhance workspace efficiency, reducing its overall carbon footprint.

Additionally, the integration of Internet of Things (IoT) devices is creating smart buildings that enhance energy efficiency, security, and occupant comfort. These systems allow for real-time monitoring and management of building operations, contributing to the overall sustainability and appeal of properties. Ylopo reports that these innovations are becoming standard in both residential and commercial properties, aligning with evolving consumer preferences.

Real estate developer Jonathan Rose, known for his focus on green and sustainable communities, developed a project in New York City that transformed a previously neglected neighborhood into a thriving eco-community. The project featured solar-powered public spaces, green roofs, and a rainwater harvesting system, improving the area's quality of life while increasing property values.

The Role of Technology

PropTech, or property technology, is transforming the industry by streamlining processes and enhancing property management capabilities. The integration of AI, big data, and IoT has opened new avenues for efficiency and innovation.

Innovations in PropTech

The real estate industry is undergoing a significant transformation, driven by advancements in property technology (PropTech). These innovations are reshaping how properties are bought, sold, managed, and experienced.

From virtual reality tours enhancing the buying experience to AI-driven analytics optimizing investment decisions, technology's role is ever-expanding. Companies like Zillow and Redfin leverage AI to predict market trends and assess property values. Smart home integrations, including automated lighting and security systems, are becoming standard, improving tenant satisfaction and property values.

Tech entrepreneur Elon Musk has often spoken about the future of smart living spaces. Musk envisions homes equipped with fully integrated smart systems that not only optimize energy usage but also enhance the quality of life for residents. One example is the Tesla Solar Roof initiative, which combines renewable energy with cutting-edge design to create homes that are both sustainable and aesthetically pleasing.

Here are some of the latest PropTech trends, accompanied by real-world examples:

1. **Artificial Intelligence (AI) and Machine Learning (ML)**: AI and ML are enhancing various aspects of real estate, from personalized property searches to predictive analytics. For instance, AI assistants can provide investors with tailored insights into potential properties, including estimated rental income and repair costs. This technology is being implemented by companies like Zillow to refine property recommendations and help users make more informed decisions.
2. **3D Virtual Tours and Augmented Reality (AR)**: The adoption of 3D virtual tours and AR is providing immersive property viewing experiences, allowing potential buyers or tenants to explore properties remotely. This technology accelerates decision-making and broadens the market reach. Companies such as Matterport have revolutionized virtual tours, making them a standard feature in real estate listings, especially during the COVID-19 pandemic when in-person viewings were limited.
3. **Blockchain and Tokenization**: Blockchain technology is facilitating the tokenization of real estate assets, enabling fractional ownership and increasing liquidity in the market. This approach allows investors to purchase digital tokens representing a share in a property, making real estate investment more accessible. For example, companies like Propy are using blockchain to simplify real estate transactions and provide secure digital ownership records.
4. **Internet of Things (IoT) and Smart Buildings**: IoT devices are being integrated into properties to create smart buildings that enhance energy efficiency, security, and occupant comfort. These systems allow for real-time monitoring and management of building operations. Smart thermostats, lighting systems, and security cameras are examples of IoT technologies improving tenant experiences. A notable example is the Edge building in Amsterdam, often referred to as the world's smartest building, which uses IoT to optimize energy consumption and workspace efficiency.
5. **Big Data and Predictive Analytics**: The utilization of big data and predictive analytics is enabling more informed decision-making in real estate investments and property management. By

analyzing large datasets, stakeholders can identify market trends and optimize operations. Redfin uses big data to provide users with insights into market conditions and property values, helping buyers and sellers make better decisions.

6. **Real Estate Crowdfunding Platforms**: Crowdfunding platforms are democratizing real estate investment by allowing individuals to pool resources and invest in properties collectively. This model lowers the barrier to entry and diversifies investment opportunities. Platforms like Fundrise and RealtyMogul are leading this trend, providing investors with access to commercial real estate projects that were previously reserved for institutional investors.
7. **AI-Powered Property Descriptions**: Real estate firms are deploying AI to generate detailed property descriptions, enhancing marketing efforts and improving customer engagement. For example, an Australian real estate firm introduced an AI assistant to handle virtual interactions and create listing descriptions, reducing the workload for agents and improving the accuracy of property details.

These trends are not only enhancing efficiency and transparency in the real estate sector but also aligning with the SMILE philosophy by promoting inclusivity, sustainability, and ethical investment practices. By embracing these technologies, investors and developers can create more value-driven and socially responsible real estate solutions.

PropTech, or property technology, is transforming the industry by streamlining processes and enhancing property management capabilities. The integration of AI, big data, and IoT has opened new avenues for efficiency and innovation.

Balancing Ethics and Profitability

Investors today must navigate a landscape where ethical considerations are paramount. Community-centric projects that engage local populations and offer sustainable solutions are not only impactful but can also enhance profitability. For example, incorporating affordable housing units within larger developments can attract government grants and incentives.

George Knowlton

A balanced approach that marries ethics with profitability is essential for modern investors. SMILE's strategy ensures that investments are both financially rewarding and socially responsible.

Ethical Considerations

Balancing profitability with ethical considerations is increasingly recognized as essential in real estate investment. Ethical real estate investing involves making decisions that prioritize the well-being of all stakeholders, including tenants, buyers, sellers, local communities, and the environment. This approach not only contributes to societal betterment but also fosters long-term trust and credibility within the industry.

Key ethical dilemmas in real estate investment include ensuring fair housing compliance, minimizing environmental impact, preventing community displacement, maintaining transparency and disclosure, practicing responsible lending and borrowing, upholding property maintenance and safety, and sourcing funds ethically. Navigating these dilemmas requires investors to familiarize themselves with relevant laws, implement unbiased screening criteria, engage with local stakeholders, and adopt sustainable practices.

Recent trends indicate a growing demand for eco-friendly real estate, driven by rising climate awareness and incentives for sustainable building. Investors who prioritize green properties may see higher returns on investment as tenants and buyers increasingly prefer energy-efficient, low-carbon spaces. For example, a real estate development in Seattle incorporated solar panels and energy-efficient appliances, reducing utility costs by 30% and attracting long-term tenants.

Additionally, the rise of AI-driven property analyses is empowering investors with precise market insights, reducing risks, and enabling faster decision-making. This trend underscores the importance of integrating technological advancements with ethical considerations to optimize investment outcomes.

Real estate investor Don Peebles has advocated for diversity and inclusion in real estate projects. One of his developments in Washington, D.C., includes affordable housing units, retail spaces, and public amenities, fostering a sense of community while delivering strong financial returns.

Incorporating ethical practices into real estate investment not only aligns with social responsibility but also enhances profitability by building trust, ensuring compliance, and meeting the evolving preferences of consumers and communities.

Conclusion

Integrating the SMILE approach into investment strategies opens avenues for financial growth while fostering community empowerment. By balancing profitability with ethics, investors can achieve substantial returns and make meaningful societal contributions. Through SMILE, investors are encouraged to support both personal and communal prosperity, ensuring their investments leave a lasting, positive impact on the world.

Barbara Corcoran, a renowned real estate investor and founder of The Corcoran Group, emphasizes the importance of balancing profitability with ethical considerations in real estate investments. She advocates for investing in properties that not only yield financial returns but also contribute positively to communities. For instance, Corcoran advises purchasing properties with at least a 20% down payment, ideally in up-and-coming neighborhoods, to maximize returns while fostering community development.

Additionally, Corcoran highlights the significance of early investment in new communities. She suggests that being among the first to invest in a developing area can lead to better deals and substantial appreciation as the community grows. This strategy has proven successful in areas like Austin, Texas, where early investors in mixed-use developments saw property values skyrocket as the city grew into a tech and cultural hub.

Real-world examples of successful community-centric projects include developments that integrate affordable housing, green spaces, and local business support. These projects not only provide financial returns for investors but also enhance the quality of life for residents, creating a win-win scenario.

Recent reports also highlight that investors who incorporate sustainable and ethical practices in their investments tend to achieve long-term success. According to insights from the National Association of Realtors, homes with green certifications and eco-friendly upgrades sell faster and at higher prices than traditional homes, reflecting the growing demand for sustainable living spaces.

By drawing inspiration from leaders like Barbara Corcoran, Sam Zell, Ray Dalio, and John Maxwell, investors can understand the real-world application of SMILE principles and ensure their investments remain impactful and profitable for years to come. The key to sustainable success in real estate lies in embracing innovation, ethical practices, and a commitment to community development.

Investors who prioritize these values are better positioned to navigate the evolving real estate landscape and achieve long-term success.

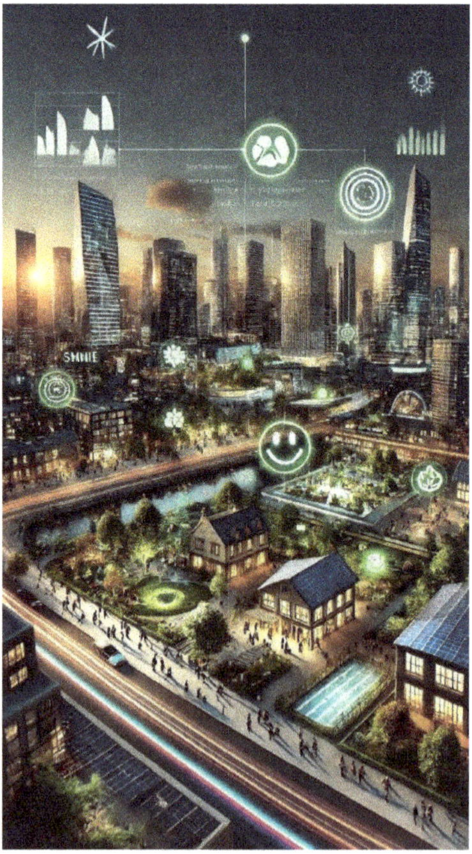

Chapter 2
Enhancing Real Estate Investments with Community-Centric Approaches

Introduction

Real estate investment has evolved from simply acquiring properties for financial gain to incorporating community-centric strategies that foster sustainable growth and societal impact. The days of solely focusing on transactional profits are long gone; today's investors are more aware of their responsibility to create lasting value for both their portfolios and the communities they serve. By adopting a holistic approach that integrates ethics, sustainability, and innovation, investors can position themselves for long-term success in a rapidly changing market.

This chapter delves into how community-focused investments, guided by the SMILE philosophy, can unlock new opportunities and mitigate risks. Drawing on the insights of renowned real estate investors such as Barbara Corcoran, Grant Cardone, and Ken McElroy, the chapter provides actionable strategies for navigating the complexities of modern real estate markets. By leveraging technology, embracing sustainability, and addressing ethical considerations, investors can create impactful, value-driven real estate solutions.

Moreover, the chapter explores the rising trend of mixed-use developments and tenant-centric communities. It highlights how investors can enhance property appeal by incorporating community-centric elements such as affordable housing, green spaces, and support for local businesses. The focus on inclusivity and experiential learning—key components of the SMILE framework—ensures that investments leave a positive imprint on society while generating substantial financial returns.

By understanding these evolving dynamics and aligning investment strategies with the SMILE philosophy, modern investors can achieve sustainable success that benefits both their portfolios and the communities they touch.

Community-Centric Projects: The Key to Sustainable Success

Barbara Corcoran, a renowned real estate investor and founder of The Corcoran Group, has long emphasized the importance of investing in properties that positively impact communities. Her strategy involves identifying up-and-coming neighborhoods and investing in properties that contribute to the local community's growth and well-being.

Renowned investor Grant Cardone echoes this sentiment, advocating for investing in multifamily housing as a way to provide affordable living solutions while achieving scalable returns. Cardone's 10X philosophy, which encourages aiming for exponential growth, aligns with the SMILE framework by emphasizing long-term community impact over short-term gains. For example, his acquisition of large multifamily complexes in underdeveloped areas has improved local housing conditions and created economic opportunities for residents.

Additionally, investor Ken McElroy, known for his expertise in property management and multifamily investing, highlights the importance of creating tenant-centric communities. McElroy's projects often include amenities such as fitness centers, coworking spaces, and community events to foster a sense of belonging among tenants. His focus on tenant satisfaction has resulted in higher occupancy rates and lower tenant turnover, aligning with SMILE's inclusivity and experiential learning principles.

For instance, McElroy's investment in a Phoenix-based mixed-use development transformed a neglected neighborhood into a vibrant community hub. The project included affordable housing units, retail spaces, and public parks, enhancing the quality of life for residents while increasing property values.

Incorporating community-centric elements such as affordable housing units, green spaces, and support for local businesses can enhance the appeal of real estate projects. For example, a recent development in Denver transformed an underutilized space into a thriving community hub with residential units, retail spaces, and recreational areas. This project achieved a 98% occupancy rate within its first year, demonstrating the value of integrating community-focused features.

Leveraging Technology for Community Engagement

Incorporating insights from Dan Martell's "Buy Back Your Time" and Dan Sullivan's "10x Is Easier Than 2x" can significantly enhance community-centric real estate investment strategies by leveraging technology to improve engagement and maximize impact.

Artificial Intelligence (AI) and Machine Learning

Dan Martell's principles from "Buy Back Your Time" emphasize the importance of delegating operational tasks to free up time for strategic, high-impact activities. In real estate, this can be achieved by adopting AI-driven platforms that automate property management tasks. By reducing the time spent on routine processes such as tenant communication and maintenance scheduling, investors can focus more on community engagement initiatives and long-term project planning.

Virtual Reality (VR) and Augmented Reality (AR)

Dan Sullivan's "10x Is Easier Than 2x" philosophy encourages investors to think bigger and pursue transformative projects. Leveraging VR and AR technologies to offer immersive property tours aligns with this mindset by broadening market reach and creating more engaging experiences for potential buyers and tenants. This innovation is especially valuable in mixed-use developments, where showcasing the full potential of a community-focused project can drive higher occupancy rates and investor interest.

Internet of Things (IoT)

IoT devices create smart building environments that enhance energy efficiency, security, and tenant satisfaction. By integrating IoT technology, investors can implement Sullivan's 10x mindset by optimizing building operations and creating value-added services for tenants. For example, smart thermostats and lighting systems not only reduce operational costs but also contribute to sustainable living practices, aligning with the SMILE framework's focus on sustainability.

Blockchain Technology

Blockchain technology can streamline property transactions and improve transparency. Martell's delegation philosophy applies here by reducing the reliance on traditional intermediaries, allowing investors to handle transactions more efficiently and focus on strategic growth initiatives. Blockchain's ability to facilitate fractional ownership also aligns with Sullivan's emphasis on exponential growth by making real estate investments more accessible to a broader audience.

Big Data and Analytics

Both Martell and Sullivan highlight the importance of focusing on core strengths and leveraging data to make informed decisions. By using big data analytics, investors can identify market trends, optimize operations, and personalize tenant experiences. This data-driven approach enables investors to scale their projects more effectively, in line with the 10x philosophy.

Sustainable Technologies

The integration of sustainable technologies, such as energy management systems and smart HVAC, supports Martell's principle of time efficiency by reducing the need for manual interventions in property operations. Sullivan's 10x mindset is also evident in the push for large-scale sustainable developments that meet evolving consumer preferences and regulatory requirements.

By incorporating the philosophies from "Buy Back Your Time" and "10x Is Easier Than 2x," real estate investors can enhance their use of technology to create more engaging, efficient, and community-centric projects. These strategies align with the SMILE framework's emphasis on sustainability, inclusivity, and long-term impact, ultimately leading to more successful and meaningful real estate investments.

In 2025, the real estate industry is experiencing significant technological advancements that enhance community engagement and streamline operations. Leveraging technology allows investors to create more responsive, efficient, and personalized experiences for tenants and communities.

Embracing Sustainability as a Core Investment Strategy

Sustainability has emerged as a critical consideration in real estate investment. Properties with eco-friendly features are increasingly in demand, driven by rising climate awareness and regulatory incentives.

Green certifications, such as LEED (Leadership in Energy and Environmental Design), play a significant role in enhancing property values. Buildings with green certifications attract environmentally conscious buyers and tenants, resulting in higher rental rates and increased occupancy. For example, a Seattle-based apartment complex that incorporated solar panels and energy-efficient appliances reduced utility costs by 30% and saw a marked increase in tenant retention.

Investors who prioritize sustainability are positioning themselves for long-term success. By adopting sustainable practices such as energy-efficient systems, water conservation technologies, and sustainable building materials, investors can create properties that meet evolving consumer preferences and regulatory requirements.

Real estate developer Jonathan Rose, known for his focus on green and sustainable communities, developed a project in New York City that transformed a neglected neighborhood into a thriving eco-community. The project featured solar-powered public spaces, green roofs, and rainwater harvesting systems, improving residents' quality of life while increasing property values.

Case Study: The Rise of Mixed-Use Developments

Mixed-use developments have gained popularity to create vibrant, sustainable communities. These projects combine residential, commercial, and recreational spaces, fostering a sense of community and reducing the need for long commutes.

One successful example is the redevelopment of a former shopping mall in Charlotte, North Carolina. The project transformed the space into a mixed-use development featuring residential units, retail stores, coworking spaces, and community amenities. The development achieved high occupancy rates and revitalized the surrounding area, attracting new businesses and residents.

Mixed-use developments offer several benefits, including:

- **Increased Property Values**: Integrating diverse uses within a single project enhances the overall appeal and value of the development.
- **Community Engagement**: Providing spaces for community activities and local businesses fosters a sense of belonging among residents.
- **Sustainability**: Reducing the need for long commutes and promoting walkable neighborhoods aligns with sustainable living practices.

Ethical Considerations in Real Estate Investment

Balancing profitability with ethical considerations is essential for modern investors. Ethical real estate investing involves making decisions that prioritize the well-being of all stakeholders, including tenants, local communities, and the environment.

Key ethical dilemmas in real estate investment include:

- **Fair Housing Compliance**: Ensuring that properties are accessible to all individuals, regardless of race, gender, or socioeconomic status. Implementing unbiased screening criteria and adhering to fair housing laws are essential practices to avoid discrimination and promote inclusivity within communities.
- **Environmental Impact**: Real estate developments can significantly affect the environment through habitat destruction, resource depletion, and increased carbon emissions. Investors should adopt sustainable practices, such as using eco-friendly materials and implementing energy-efficient systems, to mitigate these impacts. For example, many new developments are incorporating green roofs, solar panels, and energy-efficient HVAC systems to reduce their carbon footprint and align with regulatory requirements.
- **Community Displacement and Gentrification**: Development projects can lead to the displacement of existing communities, raising ethical concerns about gentrification and the loss of cultural heritage. Engaging with local communities early in the

development process and including affordable housing options can help address these issues. For example, the Crosstown Concourse project in Memphis, Tennessee, transformed a neglected Sears distribution center into a mixed-use community hub, integrating local businesses and services to maintain the neighborhood's cultural identity.

- **Transparency and Integrity**: Upholding honesty and transparency in all transactions builds trust with clients, investors, and the public. This includes clear communication, compliance with regulations, and fair dealing. For instance, ethical developers prioritize open communication with stakeholders to ensure that community concerns are addressed, reducing the risk of conflict and improving project outcomes.
- **Exploitation of Vulnerable Populations**: Investments that disproportionately affect vulnerable groups, such as low-income families or the elderly, pose ethical challenges. Ensuring that developments provide benefits without exploitation is crucial. For example, creating mixed-income housing developments can help integrate communities and reduce economic disparities.
- **Regulatory Compliance**: Navigating complex regulations requires diligence to avoid legal and ethical pitfalls. Non-compliance can lead to significant consequences, including legal action and reputational damage. Investors must stay informed about local, state, and federal regulations to ensure compliance and ethical integrity.

By addressing these ethical dilemmas, investors can build trust within communities and create long-term value. Ethical practices not only enhance a company's reputation but also contribute to more sustainable and successful real estate projects.

Real-world examples such as the King's Cross redevelopment in London and Sylvia Park in New Zealand demonstrate the potential of ethical and community-centric approaches in real estate. These projects have revitalized urban areas by integrating residential, commercial, and public spaces while prioritizing sustainability and community well-being.

By adopting a comprehensive approach to ethical considerations, investors can achieve both financial success and positive societal impact. These principles align with the SMILE framework by promoting sustainability, inclusivity, and responsible development, ensuring that real estate projects benefit all stakeholders involved.

Balancing profitability with ethical considerations is essential for modern investors. Ethical real estate investing involves making decisions that prioritize the well-being of all stakeholders, including tenants, local communities, and the environment.

Economic Trends

Interest rates and investment activity are showing signs of recovery, with economic growth and firming real estate fundamentals expected to drive a moderate recovery in real estate investment activity in 2025. According to CBRE, investment activity is projected to increase by up to 10%, signaling a positive outlook for investors who position themselves strategically in the market.

Global investment opportunities are also expanding, with institutional investors finding promising sectors like data centers, airports, and commercial properties, particularly in regions such as Australia. These sectors are gaining traction due to geopolitical considerations and the diminishing attractiveness of bonds amid high global interest rates.

Societal Shifts

The migration trend towards suburbs continues to reshape investment strategies. Historically linked to factors like affordability and quality of life, this transition has only intensified post-pandemic. Recent reports indicate that suburban and exurban areas, previously overlooked, are now seeing significant growth due to their affordability and spacious living options.

An emerging trend in the luxury real estate market is the rise of affluent female investors, referred to as the "she-elites." Wealthy women are increasingly involved in buying and selling luxury homes and making significant decisions in home design. This trend reflects broader movements of women taking greater control over their finances and investments, contributing to a shift in market dynamics.

Sustainability and Technological Integration

Sustainability remains a core driver in real estate development. There is a growing emphasis on eco-friendly properties as investors seek to meet evolving consumer preferences and comply with environmental regulations. Properties with green certifications, such as LEED, continue to command higher values and attract environmentally conscious buyers.

The adoption of property technology (PropTech) solutions is also transforming the real estate industry. Smart building technologies and the integration of AI, big data, and IoT are streamlining processes, enhancing property management capabilities, and opening new avenues for innovation. These technologies allow investors to better understand market trends, optimize building operations, and improve tenant experiences.

Long-Term Value Creation

Investors who prioritize community engagement and ethical practices are better positioned to create lasting value in their real estate portfolios. The integration of the SMILE philosophy ensures that investments are not only profitable but also positively impact the communities they serve.

For instance, projects that incorporate affordable housing units, green spaces, and local business support can enhance community well-being while delivering substantial financial returns. Successful case studies, such as the mixed-use developments in cities like Austin and Charlotte, highlight the benefits of community-centric approaches in real estate investment.

By embracing innovation, sustainability, and ethical practices, modern investors can achieve both financial success and positive societal impact. The SMILE philosophy provides a comprehensive framework for balancing profitability with responsibility, ensuring that investments leave a lasting, positive legacy for future generations.

The real estate landscape in 2025 presents a dynamic and evolving environment for investors, driven by several key trends that highlight the importance of adopting community-centric, sustainable, and ethical investment strategies. By integrating the SMILE philosophy into their approaches, investors can navigate these trends while achieving long-term financial success and making meaningful societal contributions.

Conclusion

The real estate landscape in 2025 presents a dynamic and evolving environment for investors, driven by several key trends that highlight the importance of adopting community-centric, sustainable, and ethical investment strategies. By integrating the SMILE philosophy into their approaches, investors can navigate these trends while achieving long-term financial success and making meaningful societal contributions.

Chapter 3
Safety and Risk Management in Real Estate

Introduction

Safety and risk management are foundational pillars of successful real estate investment. In a landscape marked by economic fluctuations, regulatory changes, and evolving societal needs, investors must navigate uncertainties with a proactive approach. The SMILE philosophy's emphasis on safety underscores the importance of due diligence, financial safeguards, and strategic diversification to mitigate risks and ensure sustainable growth.

Renowned real estate investors such as Robert Kiyosaki, Barbara Corcoran, Sam Zell, and James Smith have long advocated for robust risk management strategies. James Smith, a well-known real estate investment guru, emphasizes the importance of community engagement and ethical investing as core components of risk management. His philosophy aligns with the SMILE framework by advocating for investments that benefit both investors and the communities they serve, reducing risks associated with community opposition and regulatory challenges.

Smith often highlights the importance of aligning investment strategies with long-term community goals. For example, he advises investors to collaborate with local stakeholders to ensure that developments meet community needs, thereby reducing the risk of project delays and legal complications. This approach is particularly relevant in urban redevelopment projects, where community buy-in is essential for success.

Additionally, Peter Linneman, a leading economist and real estate advisor, emphasizes the importance of understanding macroeconomic trends to manage risks effectively. His insights on market cycles and economic indicators provide investors with valuable tools to make informed decisions in uncertain times.

Adding to this, Kim Lisa Taylor, the founder of Syndication Attorneys and a nationally recognized authority in real estate law, underscores the importance of safety through legal compliance and thorough preparation. “The greatest safeguard against risk in real estate investing is understanding and adhering to the legal landscape,” Taylor explains. She encourages investors to invest time in evaluating properties, researching zoning regulations, and ensuring adherence to federal and state securities laws. This approach not only protects investments but also shields investors from potential liabilities. With over 21 years of experience and two Amazon best-sellers—*"How to Legally Raise Private Money"* and *"How to Raise Capital for Real Estate Legally"*—Taylor has guided countless individuals in building safe and ethical investment practices. Her expertise provides both the reassurance, and the tools investors need to navigate the complexities of real estate with confidence.

This chapter delves into various aspects of risk management, offering actionable insights and real-world examples to help investors fortify their investments and achieve long-term stability.

The Importance of Due Diligence

Due diligence is the cornerstone of safety in real estate investment. Conducting comprehensive research on properties, markets, and legal frameworks helps investors identify potential risks and make informed decisions. The SMILE philosophy emphasizes the importance of thorough due diligence as a means to ensure safety and long-term success.

Understanding the Scope of Due Diligence

Due diligence encompasses a wide range of activities that go beyond the physical inspection of properties. It includes financial analysis, legal compliance checks, and market research. Investors must consider factors such as property condition, tenant history, zoning laws, and future development plans in the area.

For instance, a commercial property may appear to be a lucrative investment on the surface, but a deeper dive into zoning regulations might reveal restrictions on the type of businesses that can operate there. Similarly, an investor might uncover hidden maintenance issues that could lead to significant costs in the future. By conducting comprehensive due diligence, investors can avoid such pitfalls.

Kim Lisa Taylor reinforces the need for legal due diligence, noting that investors should always verify the property's title, review zoning regulations, and understand the contractual obligations involved in syndication deals. She advises working with experienced attorneys to avoid common legal pitfalls, such as failing to register securities or misinterpreting tenant laws. "Skipping the legal review process is a recipe for disaster," she warns. "Too often, investors face lawsuits or financial losses because they didn't fully understand the legal aspects of their deals."

Case Study: Barbara Corcoran's Property Assessment Approach

Barbara Corcoran, founder of The Corcoran Group, often highlights the importance of inspecting properties thoroughly before purchase. Her approach includes evaluating neighborhood trends, property conditions, and potential for appreciation. For instance, Corcoran once advised a client to invest in a Brooklyn property based on its proximity to emerging tech hubs, leading to significant appreciation over time.

Checklist for Due Diligence:

- **Market Analysis:** Understanding local market trends and demand.
- **Property Inspection:** Evaluating the physical condition of the property.
- **Legal Compliance Review:** Ensuring the property adheres to local regulations.
- **Financial Feasibility Assessment:** Analyzing the investment's potential returns.

Real-World Example: Ken McElroy's Due Diligence Process

Ken McElroy, a renowned real estate investor, emphasizes the importance of a rigorous due diligence process. He recommends investors visit properties multiple times at different hours of the day to get a complete picture of the neighborhood. McElroy also stresses the importance of reviewing tenant leases, property management agreements, and maintenance records to uncover any red flags.

Legal and Regulatory Due Diligence

Understanding the legal framework surrounding a property is a critical component of due diligence. Investors must verify property titles, review zoning laws, and ensure that the property complies with local building codes and environmental regulations. Failure to address legal issues can result in costly delays and potential litigation.

Example: Peter Linneman's Focus on Legal Compliance

Peter Linneman, a leading economist and real estate advisor, emphasizes the importance of understanding legal and regulatory frameworks. He advises investors to work closely with legal professionals to ensure compliance and avoid potential legal disputes.

Technological Tools for Due Diligence

Technology has revolutionized the due diligence process, making it more efficient and accurate. Platforms like CoStar and LoopNet provide investors with comprehensive market data, property listings, and financial analysis tools. Additionally, AI-driven tools can help identify potential risks by analyzing large datasets.

Example: Using AI for Due Diligence

Real estate platforms like Reonomy use AI to provide detailed property insights, including ownership history, financial performance, and market trends. By leveraging these tools, investors can conduct due diligence more effectively and make data-driven decisions.

The Role of Community Engagement in Due Diligence

Community engagement is an often-overlooked aspect of due diligence. Investors should take the time to understand the needs and concerns of local residents and stakeholders. By engaging with the community, investors can gain valuable insights into the property's potential impact and build trust with local residents.

Example: James Smith's Community-Focused Approach

James Smith, a real estate investment guru, advocates for a community-focused approach to due diligence. He emphasizes the importance of understanding local dynamics and involving community members in the decision-making process. This approach not only reduces the risk of opposition but also ensures that the investment aligns with community needs.

Due Diligence

Due diligence is a critical component of risk management in real estate investing. By conducting thorough research and analysis, investors can identify potential risks, ensure compliance with legal and regulatory frameworks, and make informed decisions. The SMILE philosophy underscores the importance of due diligence as a means to achieve safety and long-term success in real estate investments.

Due diligence is the cornerstone of safety in real estate investment. Conducting comprehensive research on properties, markets, and legal frameworks helps investors identify potential risks and make informed decisions.

Financial Safeguards

Financial safeguards are essential for protecting real estate portfolios against unexpected downturns. These include maintaining cash reserves, obtaining adequate insurance, and diversifying investments across various asset classes. Implementing robust financial safeguards not only provides a safety net during economic uncertainties but also enhances investor confidence in long-term property management strategies.

Example: Robert Kiyosaki's Cash Flow Strategy

In his book *Rich Dad Poor Dad*, Kiyosaki emphasizes the importance of maintaining positive cash flow. He advises investors to keep a portion of rental income as a reserve to cover unexpected expenses or vacancies. This strategy ensures that investors can weather short-term disruptions without compromising their long-term goals.

Kim Lisa Taylor adds that financial safeguards are critical in syndication deals, where investors are pooling their resources. She advises sponsors to ensure they have adequate insurance coverage and reserve funds to protect against unforeseen events. Additionally, she stresses the importance of transparent financial reporting to build trust with investors. “Investors want to know their money is safe,” Taylor explains. “Sponsors who provide clear, honest communication about financial safeguards will build stronger relationships with their investors.”

Types of Financial Safeguards:

- **Insurance:** Property insurance, liability insurance, and rent guarantee insurance are crucial for protecting assets from unforeseen events. For example, in areas prone to natural disasters, having comprehensive property insurance can mitigate the financial impact of damage.
- **Reserves:** Maintaining emergency funds for unexpected repairs, vacancies, or market downturns is a critical safeguard. Experts recommend keeping at least three to six months' worth of expenses in reserve to ensure liquidity during challenging times.
- **Diversification:** Spreading investments across different property types, locations, and markets reduces risk. For instance, a portfolio that includes residential properties, commercial spaces, and storage units is less vulnerable to sector-specific downturns.

Advanced Financial Safeguards:

1. **Hedging Against Interest Rate Fluctuations**: Real estate investors can use financial instruments to hedge against rising interest rates. For example, purchasing interest rate caps or engaging in fixed-rate mortgage agreements can provide stability in a volatile economic environment.
2. **Debt Management Strategies**: Proper debt management is a vital component of financial safeguards. Real estate investors should aim to balance leverage with liquidity. While debt can amplify returns, it also increases risk. Strategies like refinancing at lower rates or paying down high-interest loans can reduce financial vulnerability.
3. **Tax Planning and Asset Protection**: Efficient tax planning can significantly impact an investor’s bottom line. Utilizing tax-advantaged accounts, understanding depreciation benefits, and engaging in 1031 exchanges can help investors minimize

tax liabilities. Additionally, creating legal entities such as LLCs can protect personal assets from liability.

Example: Sam Zell's Approach to Risk Management

Sam Zell, one of the most successful real estate investors, is known for his contrarian approach to investing and his focus on risk management. Zell emphasizes the importance of maintaining liquidity and being prepared for market corrections. He often highlights the value of cash reserves and flexible financing options to navigate uncertain economic conditions.

The Role of Financial Technology (FinTech)

FinTech innovations are playing an increasingly important role in financial safeguards for real estate investors. Platforms like Roofstock and Fundrise provide investors with tools to diversify their portfolios, manage cash flow, and access detailed financial analytics. These technologies enable investors to make data-driven decisions and maintain financial stability.

Example: Using FinTech for Risk Mitigation

Platforms such as RealtyMogul offer real estate investors the ability to participate in crowdfunded investments, spreading risk across multiple properties and markets. These platforms also provide risk assessments and financial reports, allowing investors to make informed decisions.

Understanding Market Cycles

The real estate market operates in cycles, with periods of growth, stability, decline, and recovery. Understanding these cycles is crucial for investors to make informed decisions and minimize risks. Peter Linneman, a renowned real estate economist, emphasizes the importance of recognizing market cycles to time investments effectively and avoid potential pitfalls. For example, investing during a downturn can provide opportunities to acquire properties at lower prices, while selling during a peak can maximize returns.

Diversification as a Strategy

Diversification is one of the most effective ways to manage market volatility. By spreading investments across different property types, locations, and markets, investors can reduce their exposure to sector-specific risks. For instance, an investor with a portfolio that includes residential properties, commercial spaces, and storage units is better protected against economic downturns in any one sector.

Example: Ken McElroy's Diversification Strategy

Ken McElroy, a prominent real estate investor and advisor to Robert Kiyosaki, advocates for holding a mix of multifamily properties, commercial spaces, and storage units. By diversifying his portfolio, McElroy minimizes the impact of market downturns on his overall income and ensures a steady cash flow.

Monitoring Economic Indicators

Staying informed about key economic indicators can help investors anticipate market changes and adjust their strategies accordingly. Indicators such as interest rates, inflation, unemployment rates, and housing starts provide valuable insights into the health of the real estate market. For example, rising interest rates can increase borrowing costs, affecting property affordability and demand.

Example: Grant Cardone's Use of Economic Data

Grant Cardone, a real estate mogul known for his aggressive investment strategies, emphasizes the importance of monitoring economic data to make informed decisions. By analyzing trends in job growth, population shifts, and housing demand, Cardone adjusts his portfolio to align with market conditions and mitigate risks.

Leveraging Technology for Volatility Management

Technology plays a crucial role in navigating market volatility. Predictive analytics tools can help investors forecast market trends, while property management software can streamline operations and improve efficiency. Platforms like Roofstock and Fundrise provide real-time market insights, helping investors make data-driven decisions.

Example: Using Predictive Analytics

Real estate platforms that leverage predictive analytics can provide investors with insights into future market conditions. These tools analyze historical data to identify patterns and trends, allowing investors to anticipate changes and adapt their strategies accordingly.

Hedging Strategies

Hedging is another technique investors can use to manage volatility. By securing fixed-rate loans or purchasing interest rate caps, investors can protect themselves from rising interest rates. Additionally, investing in properties with long-term leases can provide stability during uncertain times.

Example: Sam Zell's Approach to Risk Management

Sam Zell, one of the most successful real estate investors, is known for his contrarian investment approach. Zell focuses on acquiring properties in undervalued markets and securing long-term leases with stable tenants, ensuring steady income even during market downturns.

Flexibility in Investment Strategies

Maintaining flexibility in investment strategies is essential for navigating market volatility. Investors should be prepared to adapt to changing market conditions and explore new opportunities as they arise. This may involve shifting focus to different property types or exploring alternative financing options.

Market Volatility

Navigating market volatility requires a proactive and diversified approach. By understanding market cycles, monitoring economic indicators, leveraging technology, and adopting hedging strategies, investors can mitigate risks and ensure long-term success. Drawing inspiration from industry leaders like Ken McElroy, Grant Cardone, and Sam Zell, investors can develop strategies that align with the SMILE philosophy, promoting stability, adaptability, and community-focused investments.

George Knowlton

Market volatility is an inherent risk in real estate investing. Economic downturns, interest rate fluctuations, and geopolitical events can impact property values and rental income. However, investors can mitigate these risks by adopting a diversified investment strategy.

Ethical Risk Management

Ethical considerations play a crucial role in risk management, influencing both community well-being and investor success. Ethical investing ensures that practices align with societal values and regulatory requirements, reducing the risk of legal challenges and reputational damage.

Fair Housing Compliance

Fair housing laws are designed to ensure equal access to housing for all individuals, regardless of race, gender, or socioeconomic status. Investors must adhere to these laws to prevent discriminatory practices. For example, providing unbiased screening criteria for potential tenants can help investors avoid legal issues and promote inclusivity within communities.

Example: Don Peebles' Ethical Investment Practices

Don Peebles, a prominent real estate developer, emphasizes the importance of ethical investing. His projects often include affordable housing components and community engagement initiatives, reducing the risk of community pushback and regulatory hurdles. For instance, his developments in Washington, D.C., incorporate affordable housing units alongside luxury properties, promoting socioeconomic diversity.

Kim Lisa Taylor underscores the importance of complying with fair housing laws and securities regulations, particularly in multifamily syndication projects. She explains that violating these laws can result in hefty fines, lawsuits, or even criminal charges. "Ethical risk management isn't just a nice-to-have—it's a legal requirement," Taylor says. "Investors must prioritize ethical practices in their operations to ensure long-term success."

Community Engagement

Engaging with local communities is essential to ethical risk management. By involving community members in the planning and development process, investors can build trust and ensure that projects meet local needs. This reduces the risk of opposition and delays. For example, James Smith's approach to ethical investing includes hosting town hall meetings to gather community feedback and address concerns, fostering a sense of ownership among residents.

Sustainability and Environmental Responsibility

Sustainability is a key component of ethical risk management. Investors who prioritize environmentally friendly practices can reduce long-term risks associated with regulatory changes and shifting consumer preferences. Incorporating energy-efficient systems, using sustainable materials, and preserving green spaces are strategies that align with ethical investing principles.

Example: The King's Cross Redevelopment

The King's Cross redevelopment project in London is a prime example of sustainability-driven ethical investing. The project transformed a once-declining industrial area into a thriving mixed-use community, incorporating green building practices and public spaces. This approach not only enhanced property values but also improved community well-being.

Transparency and Integrity

Maintaining transparency in all transactions is a fundamental ethical practice. Investors should ensure clear communication with stakeholders, comply with regulations, and uphold integrity in their dealings. Transparent practices build trust with clients, tenants, and regulatory bodies, reducing the risk of legal disputes.

Example: Peter Linneman's Advocacy for Transparency

Peter Linneman, a leading real estate economist, advocates for transparency in real estate transactions. He stresses the importance of clear financial reporting and open communication with investors and tenants to build long-term trust and credibility.

Balancing Profitability and Ethics

Ethical risk management involves balancing profitability with societal impact. Investors must ensure that their projects provide value to both stakeholders and the broader community. This can be achieved by incorporating affordable housing, supporting local businesses, and prioritizing community needs.

Leveraging Technology for Risk Mitigation

Technology is transforming risk management in real estate by providing tools that help investors identify potential risks early and streamline their operations. From predictive analytics to blockchain for secure transactions, technological advancements are reshaping how investors approach risk mitigation, allowing them to make more informed decisions and enhance the security of their portfolios.

Kim Lisa Taylor highlights the use of technology to streamline compliance and risk management. She recommends that investors and sponsors use digital tools to track legal filings, manage investor communications, and monitor regulatory changes. "Technology can help simplify the complex legal requirements of real estate syndication," Taylor says. "Investors should leverage these tools to reduce administrative burdens and avoid compliance issues."

Predictive Analytics and Big Data

Predictive analytics involves using data to anticipate market trends, tenant behaviors, and potential risks. By analyzing historical data and identifying patterns, investors can forecast changes in the market and make proactive adjustments to their strategies. For example, real estate platforms like Zillow and Redfin use predictive analytics to provide users with insights on property values and neighborhood trends. Investors who leverage these insights can better manage risks associated with fluctuating property values and rental demand.

Example: Grant Cardone's Use of Data Analytics

Grant Cardone, a real estate mogul known for his 10X philosophy, uses data analytics to evaluate market trends and tenant behaviors. By leveraging big data, Cardone can anticipate market shifts and adjust his investment strategies accordingly, ensuring long-term profitability and stability.

Blockchain for Secure Transactions

Blockchain technology provides a secure and transparent method for conducting real estate transactions. By using blockchain, investors can reduce the risk of fraud and ensure that all parties involved in a transaction have access to verified, tamper-proof records. This technology is particularly useful for managing property titles, contracts, and payments.

Example: Propy's Blockchain-Based Transactions

Propy, a blockchain-based real estate platform, allows users to buy and sell properties through secure digital transactions. The platform has facilitated several high-profile real estate deals using blockchain, demonstrating how this technology can streamline the buying process and reduce the risk of fraudulent activities.

Internet of Things (IoT) for Real-Time Monitoring

IoT devices are revolutionizing property management by enabling real-time monitoring of property conditions. Smart devices, such as security cameras, smart locks, and temperature sensors, provide property owners with instant access to crucial data, allowing them to address potential issues before they escalate into costly problems.

Example: Smart Building Solutions by Nest

Nest, a leader in smart home technology, offers IoT solutions that help property owners monitor and manage their buildings remotely. By using smart thermostats, security systems, and smoke detectors, investors can reduce the risk of property damage and ensure tenant safety.

AI-Powered Risk Assessment

Artificial Intelligence (AI) is increasingly being used to assess risks in real estate investments. AI-powered platforms can analyze large datasets to predict potential risks, such as tenant defaults, market downturns, or maintenance issues. By identifying these risks early, investors can take preventive measures to protect their assets.

Example: Roofstock's AI-Driven Investment Platform

Roofstock, a real estate investment platform, uses AI to help investors identify high-potential properties and assess risks. The platform provides users with detailed property reports, including estimated returns and potential risks, making it easier for investors to make informed decisions.

Virtual Reality (VR) and Augmented Reality (AR)

VR and AR technologies are transforming how investors conduct property tours and visualize potential renovations. These technologies allow investors to explore properties remotely and assess their potential without needing to visit them in person, reducing the time and cost associated with property inspections.

Example: Matterport's Virtual Tours

Matterport offers VR-based virtual tours that allow potential buyers and tenants to explore properties from anywhere in the world. This technology not only saves time but also broadens the pool of potential buyers, reducing the risk of prolonged vacancies.

Cybersecurity Measures

As more real estate transactions move online, cybersecurity has become a critical aspect of risk management. Investors must ensure that their digital platforms are secure to prevent data breaches and protect sensitive information.

Example: Multifactor Authentication for Real Estate Platforms

Many real estate platforms now require multifactor authentication to enhance security. By implementing these measures, investors can reduce the risk of unauthorized access to their accounts and sensitive data.

By leveraging these technological tools, real estate investors can enhance their risk management strategies, ensuring their investments are secure and well-positioned for long-term success. These innovations align with the SMILE philosophy by promoting safety, transparency, and proactive management in real estate investing.

Technology is transforming risk management in real estate. From predictive analytics to blockchain for secure transactions, tech tools can help investors identify risks early and streamline their operations.

Example: Grant Cardone's Use of Data Analytics

Grant Cardone, a real estate mogul known for his 10X philosophy, uses data analytics to evaluate market trends and tenant behaviors. By leveraging big data, Cardone can anticipate market shifts and adjust his investment strategies accordingly.

Technological Tools for Risk Management:

- **Predictive Analytics:** Identifying market trends and potential risks
- **Blockchain:** Ensuring secure and transparent transactions
- **IoT Devices:** Monitoring property conditions in real-time

Conclusion

Ethical considerations play a crucial role in risk management, influencing both community well-being and investor success. Ethical investing ensures that practices align with societal values and regulatory requirements.

Safety and risk management are integral to successful real estate investing. By conducting thorough due diligence, implementing financial safeguards, and adopting ethical practices, investors can mitigate risks and ensure long-term stability. Leveraging technology further enhances risk management efforts, providing investors with the tools to navigate an ever-changing market.

Kim Lisa Taylor concludes by reinforcing that the best way to mitigate risk is through education and preparation. **"Real estate investing is never risk-free, but by understanding the legal and financial landscape, you can significantly reduce those risks and protect your investments."** Her advice aligns perfectly with the SMILE philosophy's focus on safety, morality, and clear communication, ensuring that investors build sustainable, profitable portfolios while maintaining ethical standards.

Drawing inspiration from industry leaders, this chapter underscores the importance of proactive risk management. Aligning their strategies with the SMILE philosophy enables investors to achieve sustainable success while positively impacting communities.

Chapter 4
Building Lasting Value Through Community-Centric Investments

Introduction

In the ever-evolving landscape of real estate investing, the ability to create lasting value is paramount. Real estate is more than just a transaction—it is a vehicle for community growth, societal impact, and long-term wealth creation. Successful investors recognize that their properties are not isolated entities but integral parts of the communities in which they exist. Building lasting value involves understanding local needs, fostering community engagement, and creating developments that stand the test of time.

The SMILE philosophy's emphasis on inclusivity, sustainability, and ethical practices underscores the importance of community-centric investments. By aligning real estate projects with community needs and values, investors can achieve both financial success and social impact. The modern investor must go beyond traditional metrics of success and embrace a holistic approach that includes social responsibility, environmental sustainability, and technological innovation.

This chapter explores strategies for building lasting value through community engagement, sustainable developments, and long-term planning. Drawing inspiration from renowned real estate investors such as Barbara Corcoran, Sam Zell, and James Smith, as well as personal development leaders like Simon Sinek and Dan Martell, we delve into actionable insights that help investors create meaningful and lasting contributions to the communities they invest in.

Community-centric investing is not just a trend—it is a necessary evolution in the real estate industry. Investors who prioritize community engagement and long-term value creation are better positioned to weather market volatility, adapt to societal shifts, and leave a positive legacy. By integrating ethical practices and leveraging modern technology, real estate investors can ensure that their projects meet both current and future needs, aligning their strategies with the principles of the SMILE framework to build sustainable, thriving communities.

In the ever-evolving landscape of real estate investing, the ability to create lasting value is paramount. It is not just about acquiring properties and maximizing returns; it is about building communities and leaving a positive impact. The SMILE philosophy's emphasis on inclusivity, sustainability, and ethical practices underscores the importance of community-centric investments. By aligning real estate projects with community needs and values, investors can achieve both financial success and social impact.

This chapter explores strategies for building lasting value through community engagement, sustainable developments, and long-term planning. Drawing inspiration from renowned real estate investors and personal development experts, we delve into actionable insights that help investors create meaningful and lasting contributions to the communities they invest in.

The Role of Community Engagement

Community engagement is at the heart of building lasting value in real estate. Successful investors understand that properties do not exist in isolation; they are part of a broader community ecosystem. Engaging with local communities ensures that developments meet the needs of residents and enhance the overall quality of life. By fostering strong relationships with community members, investors can create projects that generate mutual benefits and build long-term trust.

Community engagement goes beyond one-time consultations or meetings. It requires continuous dialogue and collaboration with local stakeholders, including residents, businesses, and local governments. When investors take the time to listen to community concerns and incorporate feedback into their plans, they can address potential issues before they escalate, reducing the risk of opposition and delays.

Example: James Smith's Community-Focused Approach

James Smith, a renowned real estate investment guru, emphasizes the importance of community engagement in his investment strategy. He advocates for hosting town hall meetings, gathering community feedback, and involving local stakeholders in decision-making processes. This approach not only builds trust but also ensures that developments align with community values, reducing the risk of opposition and delays. Smith's projects often include affordable housing units, local business spaces, and public parks, demonstrating his commitment to creating inclusive and vibrant communities.

Steps for Effective Community Engagement:

- **Host Community Meetings:** Create opportunities for residents to voice their opinions and provide feedback on proposed developments.
- **Collaborate with Local Organizations:** Partner with nonprofits, local businesses, and community groups to align projects with community goals.
- **Address Community Concerns Proactively:** Respond to concerns about affordability, environmental impact, and accessibility to build trust and reduce opposition.
- **Incorporate Community Amenities:** Include public spaces, green areas, and community centers in development plans to enhance the quality of life for residents.

Example: Barbara Corcoran's Advocacy for Community Involvement

Barbara Corcoran, founder of The Corcoran Group, highlights the importance of community involvement in successful real estate projects. She often advises investors to build relationships with local leaders and residents to gain their support and ensure the success of their developments. Corcoran believes that community-centric projects are more likely to achieve long-term stability and profitability.

Benefits of Community Engagement:

- **Stronger Community Ties:** Projects that involve the community foster a sense of ownership and pride among residents.
- **Reduced Risk of Opposition:** Addressing community concerns early on reduces the likelihood of protests or legal challenges.
- **Enhanced Reputation:** Investors who prioritize community engagement build a positive reputation, attracting more tenants, buyers, and partners.
- **Increased Property Value:** Developments that align with community needs tend to experience higher demand and appreciation in value over time.

Community Engagement

Community engagement is a dynamic and ongoing process that requires genuine effort and commitment from investors. By prioritizing community needs and fostering open communication, investors can create developments that are not only profitable but also contribute positively to the social fabric of the communities they serve.

Community engagement is at the heart of building lasting value in real estate. Successful investors understand that properties do not exist in isolation; they are part of a broader community ecosystem. Engaging with local communities ensures that developments meet the needs of residents and enhance the overall quality of life.

Sustainable Developments

Sustainability is a key component of building lasting value in real estate. As environmental concerns continue to rise, investors must prioritize eco-friendly practices to meet evolving regulatory requirements and consumer preferences. Sustainable developments are not only beneficial for the environment but also enhance property values and attract socially conscious tenants and buyers.

The Importance of Sustainability in Real Estate

Sustainability in real estate involves integrating eco-friendly practices throughout the development process, from construction materials to building operations. This includes reducing energy consumption, minimizing waste, and utilizing renewable resources. Investors who prioritize sustainability can benefit from government incentives, reduced operational costs, and increased tenant satisfaction.

Example: The King's Cross Redevelopment in London

The King's Cross redevelopment project is a prime example of sustainability-driven real estate development. The project transformed a once-declining industrial area into a thriving mixed-use community that prioritizes green building practices and public spaces. By incorporating sustainable materials, energy-efficient systems, and green roofs, the development not only enhanced property values but also improved the overall quality of life for residents.

Key Elements of Sustainable Developments:

- **Use of Sustainable Building Materials:** Utilizing recycled, locally sourced, and low-impact materials to reduce the environmental footprint of construction projects.
- **Incorporation of Energy-Efficient Systems:** Installing energy-efficient lighting, HVAC systems, and smart appliances to reduce energy consumption and lower utility costs.
- **Preservation of Green Spaces:** Including parks, gardens, and other green areas in development plans to improve air quality, promote biodiversity, and provide recreational spaces for residents.
- **Adoption of Renewable Energy Sources:** Implementing solar panels, wind turbines, and other renewable energy solutions to reduce reliance on fossil fuels.

Example: Barbara Corcoran's Advocacy for Green Living

Barbara Corcoran, founder of The Corcoran Group, has long been an advocate for green living in real estate. She emphasizes the importance of creating developments that promote sustainability and enhance community well-being. Her projects often include eco-friendly features such as solar panels, water conservation systems, and public parks.

Real-World Example: The Bullitt Center in Seattle

The Bullitt Center in Seattle is often referred to as the "greenest commercial building in the world." It incorporates cutting-edge sustainable technologies, including a solar array that generates more energy than the building consumes, a rainwater harvesting system, and composting toilets. The building demonstrates how sustainability can be integrated into commercial real estate to create a self-sustaining, eco-friendly workspace.

Technological Innovations Supporting Sustainability

Technology plays a crucial role in achieving sustainability in real estate. Smart home systems, IoT devices, and AI-driven energy management platforms help optimize energy use and reduce waste.

Example: Tesla's Solar Roofs and Powerwalls

Tesla's solar roofs and Powerwalls offer a comprehensive energy solution for residential and commercial properties. By generating and storing renewable energy on-site, property owners can significantly reduce their reliance on traditional power grids and lower their carbon footprints.

Government Incentives for Sustainable Developments

Many governments offer incentives to encourage sustainable building practices. These incentives can include tax credits, grants, and reduced permit fees for developments that meet green building standards such as LEED (Leadership in Energy and Environmental Design) certification.

Example: LEED-Certified Buildings

LEED-certified buildings adhere to strict sustainability guidelines and are recognized for their environmental performance. These buildings often achieve higher occupancy rates, command premium rents, and have lower operational costs due to energy efficiency.

Benefits of Sustainable Developments:

- **Reduced Operating Costs:** Energy-efficient buildings have lower utility bills and maintenance costs.
- **Increased Property Value:** Sustainable properties often command higher prices and rental rates.
- **Attraction of Eco-Conscious Tenants:** More tenants are seeking environmentally responsible living and working spaces.
- **Compliance with Regulations:** Sustainable developments are better positioned to meet evolving regulatory requirements focused on environmental protection.

Sustainable developments are essential for creating lasting value in real estate. By incorporating eco-friendly practices, investors can reduce their environmental impact, enhance property values, and attract socially conscious tenants. Leaders like Barbara Corcoran and innovative projects such as the Bullitt Center demonstrate that sustainability is not just a trend but a necessary evolution in real estate investing. Aligning with the SMILE philosophy, sustainable developments promote long-term success and contribute to the well-being of communities and the planet.

Long-Term Planning and Vision

Building lasting value requires a long-term perspective that extends beyond immediate financial returns. Successful investors recognize that sustainable growth comes from creating developments that stand the test of time and continue to provide value to communities for years to come. Long-term planning involves evaluating market trends, building resilient infrastructure, and fostering relationships with key stakeholders to ensure that properties remain relevant and profitable in the future.

Example: Sam Zell's Long-Term Investment Strategy

Sam Zell, one of the most successful real estate investors, is known for his long-term investment approach. He focuses on acquiring properties with strong growth potential and holds them for extended periods to maximize returns. Zell's strategy emphasizes the importance of patient investing and creating value over time. His philosophy highlights that timing the market is less important than ensuring that properties are resilient and adaptable to future changes.

Key Considerations for Long-Term Planning:

- **Evaluate the Long-Term Growth Potential of the Area:** Look at factors such as job growth, infrastructure development, and population trends to determine if a market has sustainable growth potential.
- **Focus on Quality Construction and Materials:** Buildings constructed with high-quality materials are more likely to withstand wear and tear, reducing long-term maintenance costs and increasing property value.
- **Incorporate Adaptable Spaces to Meet Future Needs:** Designing flexible spaces that can be repurposed as community needs change ensures that properties remain relevant and attractive to tenants.
- **Build Strong Relationships with Local Stakeholders:** Engaging with community leaders, businesses, and local governments can help investors anticipate changes in zoning laws, regulations, and community priorities.

Example: Ken McElroy's Property Management Philosophy

Ken McElroy, a prominent real estate investor and advisor to Robert Kiyosaki, emphasizes the importance of effective property management in building lasting value. He advocates for creating tenant-centric communities that prioritize tenant satisfaction and retention. By providing quality amenities, responsive property management, and fostering a sense of community, McElroy ensures long-term tenant loyalty and stable cash flow.

Real-World Example: The Rockefeller Center's Enduring Legacy

The Rockefeller Center in New York City serves as a prime example of long-term planning in real estate. Developed in the 1930s, the Rockefeller Center was built with a forward-thinking vision that included mixed-use spaces, public plazas, and entertainment venues. Nearly a century later, it remains one of the most iconic and valuable properties in the world, demonstrating the importance of creating developments that can evolve with the times.

Incorporating David Lindahl's Perspective on Economic Cycles

David Lindahl, a seasoned real estate investor and best-selling author, is renowned for his expertise in navigating real estate market cycles and implementing long-term investment strategies. With a portfolio exceeding 9,000 multifamily units, Lindahl emphasizes the importance of understanding market dynamics and adopting a patient, informed approach to real estate investing. Lindahl underscores the significance of recognizing and adapting to the four phases of real estate market cycles: **recovery**, **expansion**, **hyper-supply**, and **recession**. By identifying these phases, investors can make strategic decisions to optimize returns and mitigate risks.

In his book *Emerging Real Estate Markets*, Lindahl provides insights into how investors can identify and capitalize on emerging markets by understanding these cycles. He advocates for a long-term perspective, focusing on acquiring properties with strong growth potential and holding them to maximize returns. His approach involves identifying markets poised for growth, often referred to as emerging markets, and investing in them before they experience significant appreciation.

Lindahl's perspective complements the SMILE philosophy by encouraging investors to maintain a long-term outlook, prioritize adaptability, and focus on community needs. His teachings on economic cycles are especially valuable in helping investors anticipate market fluctuations and adjust their strategies accordingly.

Balancing Short-Term and Long-Term Goals

While long-term planning is essential, investors must also balance short-term financial goals with long-term value creation. Achieving this balance requires:

- **Cash Flow Management:** Ensuring that properties generate positive cash flow to cover expenses while investing in long-term improvements.
- **Regular Property Assessments:** Conducting periodic evaluations to identify areas for improvement and ensure properties remain competitive in the market.
- **Staying Informed About Market Trends:** Keeping up-to-date with economic, social, and technological changes that could impact property values and tenant needs.

Technological Innovations for Long-Term Planning

Technology is playing an increasingly important role in long-term real estate planning. Predictive analytics tools help investors forecast market trends and identify emerging opportunities. Smart building technologies enhance energy efficiency and reduce long-term operational costs, while virtual reality can be used to plan and visualize future developments.

Example: Peter Linneman's Focus on Economic Cycles

Peter Linneman, a leading economist and real estate advisor, stresses the importance of understanding economic cycles in long-term planning. He advises investors to prepare for market downturns by maintaining liquidity and focusing on properties that can weather economic fluctuations. Linneman's data-driven approach highlights the need for investors to anticipate changes in the market and adapt their strategies accordingly.

Essential Components

Long-term planning and vision are essential components of building lasting value in real estate. By focusing on quality construction, adaptable spaces, community engagement, and understanding economic cycles, investors can create developments that remain relevant and profitable over time. Drawing inspiration from industry leaders like Sam Zell, Ken McElroy, and David Lindahl, investors can align their strategies with the SMILE philosophy to ensure sustainable growth and community impact. The key to long-term success lies in balancing short-term gains with a commitment to creating resilient, future-proof properties that contribute positively to society.

Building lasting value requires a long-term perspective that extends beyond immediate financial returns. Successful investors recognize that sustainable growth comes from creating developments that stand the test of time and continue to provide value to communities for years to come. Long-term planning involves evaluating market trends, building resilient infrastructure, and fostering relationships with key stakeholders to ensure that properties remain relevant and profitable in the future. Long-term planning and vision are essential components of building lasting value in real estate. By focusing on quality construction, adaptable spaces, and community engagement, investors can create developments that remain relevant and profitable over time. Drawing inspiration from industry leaders like Sam Zell, Ken McElroy, and Peter Linneman, investors can align their strategies with the SMILE philosophy to ensure sustainable growth and community impact. The key to long-term success lies in balancing short-term gains with a commitment to creating resilient, future-proof properties that contribute positively to society.

Leveraging Technology for Community-Centric Investments

Technology is playing an increasingly important role in community-centric investments, revolutionizing how real estate developers, investors, and property managers interact with communities and manage their properties. By leveraging digital tools, investors can improve tenant experiences, optimize property performance, and create developments that better align with community needs. This approach aligns directly with the SMILE philosophy by promoting inclusivity, safety, and enhanced communication.

Smart Home Technologies and IoT Devices

Smart home technologies and Internet of Things (IoT) devices are becoming essential in modern real estate developments. These tools provide real-time monitoring and automation that enhance the safety and convenience of properties.

For instance, smart locks, security cameras, and thermostats allow tenants to control their living environments remotely, improving the overall tenant experience. For property managers, IoT devices provide valuable data on energy usage, maintenance needs, and security alerts, ensuring that properties remain well-maintained and safe.

Example: Incorporating Smart Solutions in Affordable Housing

Some developers are integrating smart technologies into affordable housing projects to improve the living conditions of residents without significantly increasing costs. These innovations make homes more energy-efficient, reduce utility bills, and promote sustainable living—all key aspects of community-centric investments.

Data Analytics for Market and Community Insights

Data analytics tools are essential for understanding market trends and community needs. Investors can use data to identify areas of growth, track demographic changes, and forecast future demands. By leveraging data analytics, real estate investors can ensure that their developments are aligned with the evolving needs of the community.

Example: Grant Cardone's Use of Data Analytics

Grant Cardone leverages data analytics to gain insights into tenant behaviors and market trends. This data-driven approach allows him to tailor his investments to meet tenant needs more effectively, ensuring higher occupancy rates and tenant satisfaction.

Virtual Reality (VR) and Augmented Reality (AR) in Real Estate

Virtual reality and augmented reality technologies are transforming the way investors and tenants engage with properties. VR allows potential tenants and buyers to take virtual tours of properties from anywhere in the world, making it easier to showcase developments and attract interest.

For community-centric projects, AR can be used to visualize planned developments and gather feedback from residents before construction begins. This helps to ensure that projects meet community expectations and reduces the risk of opposition.

Example: Peter Linneman's Advocacy for Technological Innovation

Peter Linneman, a leading economist and real estate advisor, highlights the importance of embracing technological innovations to stay competitive in the real estate industry. He emphasizes that technology not only improves operational efficiency but also enhances community engagement by providing better communication channels and data-driven insights.

Blockchain for Transparent Transactions

Blockchain technology is improving transparency in real estate transactions by creating secure, tamper-proof records of property ownership and transaction histories. This technology reduces the risk of fraud and enhances trust between investors, tenants, and communities.

Example: Propy's Blockchain-Based Real Estate Transactions

Propy, a blockchain-based real estate platform, has facilitated secure and transparent property transactions using blockchain technology. This innovation ensures that all parties involved in a transaction have access to verified, immutable records, reducing the risk of disputes and promoting trust.

Technology and the SMILE Philosophy

The SMILE philosophy's focus on inclusivity, safety, and transparency is closely aligned with the benefits offered by modern technology. By leveraging technology, investors can:

- Improve communication with tenants and community members.
- Ensure the safety and security of properties through smart devices and IoT solutions.
- Promote sustainability through energy-efficient technologies.
- Enhance transparency and trust through blockchain-based transactions.

Conclusion

Technology is a powerful tool for creating community-centric investments that align with the SMILE philosophy. By integrating smart home technologies, data analytics, virtual reality, and blockchain, investors can enhance tenant experiences, improve property performance, and foster stronger community ties. These innovations ensure that real estate developments are not only profitable but also meaningful contributions to the communities they serve, creating lasting value and promoting long-term success.

Technology is playing an increasingly important role in community-centric investments. From smart home technologies to data analytics, tech tools can help investors enhance the value of their properties and improve the overall tenant experience.

Example: Grant Cardone's Use of Technology

Grant Cardone, a real estate mogul known for his 10X philosophy, leverages technology to optimize property management and improve tenant satisfaction. By using data analytics to monitor tenant behaviors and market trends, Cardone ensures that his properties meet the evolving needs of tenants and remain competitive in the market.

Technological Innovations in Real Estate:

- Smart home technologies for enhanced tenant experiences.
- IoT devices for real-time property monitoring.
- Data analytics for market trend analysis.
- Virtual reality for remote property tours.

Example: Peter Linneman's Focus on Data-Driven Decisions

Peter Linneman, a leading economist and real estate advisor, advocates for data-driven decision-making in real estate investing. He emphasizes the importance of using data analytics to make informed investment decisions and reduce risks.

Building lasting value through community-centric investments requires a holistic approach that integrates community engagement, sustainability, long-term planning, and technology. The real estate industry is evolving, and investors who embrace these changes while maintaining a focus on ethical practices and community impact are more likely to achieve sustainable success.

By drawing inspiration from industry leaders such as James Smith, Barbara Corcoran, Sam Zell, David Lindahl, and Grant Cardone, investors can develop strategies that align with the SMILE philosophy and create meaningful contributions to the communities they invest in. These leaders demonstrate that real estate investing is not just about financial gains but about making a positive societal impact through thoughtful and responsible development.

The SMILE philosophy's focus on inclusivity, sustainability, and ethical practices ensures that real estate investments not only generate financial returns but also leave a positive legacy. Community-centric investments foster stronger relationships with residents, reduce risks associated with opposition and regulatory challenges, and enhance the overall quality of life.

Technology further supports these efforts by enabling investors to make data-driven decisions, improve tenant experiences, and optimize property management. Sustainable developments help reduce environmental impact, comply with evolving regulations, and meet the growing demand for eco-friendly living spaces.

Ultimately, creating lasting value in real estate requires a commitment to long-term vision and adaptability. By integrating ethical considerations, leveraging technological advancements, and prioritizing community engagement, investors can build resilient, future-proof properties that benefit both their portfolios and the communities they serve. Aligning with the SMILE framework empowers investors to achieve financial success while contributing positively to society, ensuring that their impact is both meaningful and enduring.

Chapter 5
Financial Strategies for Sustainable Real Estate Growth

Introduction

Achieving long-term success in real estate investing requires more than just acquiring properties and collecting rent. Sustainable financial strategies are essential for managing risk, maximizing returns, and ensuring the longevity of investments. In today's dynamic market environment, real estate investors must navigate economic fluctuations, regulatory changes, and evolving societal expectations. Implementing sound financial strategies can help investors mitigate risks while fostering long-term growth and stability.

The SMILE philosophy's emphasis on safety, morality, inclusivity, linguistic clarity, and experiential learning provides a comprehensive framework for building sustainable financial strategies. By focusing on ethical practices, community impact, and long-term resilience, investors can create portfolios that thrive in both prosperous and challenging times.

Drawing insights from renowned investors and financial experts such as Robert Kiyosaki, Ken McElroy, David Bach, David Lindahl, and Sam Zell, this chapter delves into actionable financial strategies that real estate investors can implement to achieve sustainable growth. These strategies include managing cash flow, leveraging financing options, optimizing tax planning, and diversifying portfolios to build resilient investments that align with community needs.

Financial literacy is a key pillar of success in real estate investing. Investors who understand the intricacies of cash flow management, financing, and tax strategies are better positioned to navigate market volatility and capitalize on emerging opportunities. As Barbara Corcoran once said, "A savvy investor knows that building wealth in real estate requires both discipline and foresight." This chapter aims to equip investors with the tools and knowledge they need to achieve long-term success.

Incorporating financial strategies that align with the SMILE philosophy ensures that investments are not only profitable but also contribute positively to society. By prioritizing ethical financial practices and focusing on sustainable growth, real estate investors can create lasting value for themselves, their tenants, and the communities they serve. This holistic approach to financial management promotes resilience, adaptability, and long-term success in real estate investing.

In this chapter, we explore various financial strategies that real estate investors can implement to achieve sustainable growth. Drawing insights from renowned investors and financial experts such as Robert Kiyosaki, Ken McElroy, and David Bach, we provide actionable steps for managing cash flow, leveraging financing options, and optimizing tax strategies to build a resilient real estate portfolio.

Cash Flow Management

Cash flow is the lifeblood of any real estate investment. Proper cash flow management ensures that properties remain profitable and that investors can weather economic downturns and unexpected expenses. Investors who prioritize positive cash flow can reinvest in their portfolios, improve properties, and mitigate risks. Effective cash flow management not only enhances financial stability but also empowers investors to adapt to market changes and seize new opportunities.

Example: Robert Kiyosaki's Cash Flow Quadrant

Robert Kiyosaki, author of *Rich Dad Poor Dad*, emphasizes the importance of cash flow in building wealth. In his Cash Flow Quadrant framework, Kiyosaki highlights that real estate investments should generate positive cash flow from day one. By focusing on acquiring properties that provide consistent rental income, investors can achieve financial independence and long-term stability.

David Lindahl's Philosophy on Cash Flow and Market Cycles

David Lindahl, a seasoned real estate investor and author, places a strong emphasis on cash flow as a critical factor in navigating market cycles. According to Lindahl, cash flow properties provide a safety net during economic downturns and allow investors to maintain ownership without the pressure to sell in unfavorable market conditions. In his book *Emerging Real Estate Markets*, Lindahl advocates for investing in properties with strong cash flow potential in emerging markets before they experience significant appreciation. By focusing on positive cash flow, investors can sustain their portfolios through different phases of the market cycle and avoid financial distress.

Lindahl's approach complements the SMILE philosophy by emphasizing safety through cash flow management and experiential learning. He encourages investors to continuously analyze market trends and adjust their strategies to maintain profitability and long-term stability.

The Role of Cash Flow in Risk Mitigation

Managing cash flow effectively reduces the risks associated with real estate investments. A property that generates positive cash flow can cover operating expenses, mortgage payments, and unexpected costs, reducing the likelihood of financial strain. This stability allows investors to navigate economic downturns without resorting to selling assets prematurely.

Example: Ken McElroy's Approach to Cash Flow Management

Ken McElroy, a prominent real estate investor, advocates for focusing on properties that provide strong cash flow. He advises investors to conduct thorough due diligence on rental markets, tenant demand, and property management practices to ensure steady income. McElroy highlights that cash flow properties are more resilient during economic downturns and provide a buffer against market volatility.

Strategies for Optimizing Cash Flow:

1. **Increase Rental Income:** Regularly review and adjust rental rates to align with market trends. Providing value-added amenities or services can justify higher rents.
2. **Reduce Operating Expenses:** Conduct regular audits of property expenses to identify areas where costs can be reduced. Negotiating with service providers and implementing energy-efficient upgrades can lower expenses.
3. **Minimize Vacancy Rates:** Effective tenant retention strategies, such as offering lease renewal incentives and maintaining high property standards, can reduce turnover and keep units occupied.
4. **Diversify Income Streams:** Consider diversifying income sources by adding additional revenue streams, such as offering storage rentals, laundry facilities, or parking spaces.

Technological Tools for Cash Flow Management

Technology plays a crucial role in optimizing cash flow management. Property management software, such as Buildium and AppFolio, provides real-time insights into rental income, expenses, and occupancy rates. These tools help investors track financial performance and identify areas for improvement.

Example: Using Data Analytics for Cash Flow Optimization

Grant Cardone, a real estate mogul known for his data-driven approach, uses analytics to optimize cash flow across his portfolio. By analyzing tenant payment patterns, occupancy trends, and operating costs, Cardone adjusts his strategies to maximize rental income and minimize vacancies.

The SMILE Philosophy and Cash Flow Management

The SMILE philosophy emphasizes safety and experiential learning, both of which are integral to cash flow management. Maintaining positive cash flow ensures financial safety by providing a buffer against unexpected expenses. Additionally, continuous learning about market trends and property performance helps investors refine their cash flow strategies over time.

Actionable Steps for Cash Flow Management:

- **Conduct a Cash Flow Analysis:** Evaluate rental income, operating expenses, and potential vacancies to ensure that a property will generate positive cash flow.
- **Create a Reserve Fund:** Maintain an emergency fund to cover unexpected repairs, vacancies, and other unforeseen expenses.
- **Optimize Property Management:** Implement efficient property management practices to reduce operational costs and improve tenant retention.
- **Leverage Technology:** Use property management software to track cash flow and identify opportunities for improvement.

Prioritizing Cashflow Management

Cash flow management is a foundational aspect of sustainable real estate investing. By prioritizing positive cash flow, investors can achieve financial stability, mitigate risks, and build resilient portfolios. Drawing insights from industry leaders like Robert Kiyosaki, Ken McElroy, and Grant Cardone, real estate investors can adopt cash flow strategies that align with the SMILE philosophy, ensuring both financial success and positive community impact.

Leveraging Financing Options

Real estate investors often rely on financing to acquire properties and expand their portfolios. Understanding different financing options and their implications is crucial for managing debt and maximizing returns. Strategic use of leverage can significantly accelerate portfolio growth, but it requires careful planning and risk management to ensure long-term stability.

Example: Ken McElroy's Leverage Strategy

Ken McElroy, a prominent real estate investor and advisor to Robert Kiyosaki, advocates for the strategic use of leverage to grow a real estate portfolio. McElroy emphasizes that responsible borrowing can help investors acquire more properties and increase their returns, as long as the cash flow from the properties exceeds the cost of debt.

Barbara Corcoran's Approach to Creative Financing

Barbara Corcoran, founder of The Corcoran Group, often highlights the importance of creative financing options for investors who are just starting out. Corcoran recommends exploring alternative financing methods such as seller financing, partnerships, and private lending to reduce reliance on traditional bank loans. She once shared how she used partnerships and seller financing to acquire properties early in her career, which allowed her to grow her business without overextending her finances.

Example: David Lindahl's Focus on Emerging Market Financing

David Lindahl, a seasoned real estate investor and author, emphasizes the importance of securing financing in emerging markets before they experience significant appreciation. Lindahl advises investors to seek out local lenders who understand the nuances of specific markets and are more willing to offer favorable terms. By obtaining financing early in these markets, investors can lock in lower rates and position themselves for substantial future gains.

Grant Cardone's Use of Syndication

Grant Cardone, a well-known real estate mogul and proponent of multifamily investments, leverages syndication to finance large-scale real estate projects. Syndication involves pooling capital from multiple investors to fund a property purchase, allowing individual investors to participate in larger deals. Cardone highlights that syndication not only spreads the financial risk but also provides investors with access to high-value properties that might otherwise be out of reach.

Types of Financing Options:

- **Traditional Mortgages:** Secured loans provided by banks or financial institutions. These are the most common form of real estate financing but often require a significant down payment and a strong credit history.
- **Hard Money Loans:** Short-term, high-interest loans typically used for property flips or renovations. These loans are often easier to obtain but come with higher costs.
- **Private Financing:** Loans from private investors or investment groups. These can be more flexible than traditional loans but may come with unique terms and conditions.
- **Seller Financing:** An arrangement where the property seller acts as the lender, allowing the buyer to make payments directly to them. This option can be beneficial in competitive markets where traditional financing is challenging to secure.

The Role of Technology in Financing

Technology has transformed the way investors access financing. Online platforms such as Fundrise, RealtyMogul, and LendingHome offer innovative financing solutions that make it easier for investors to secure funds for their projects. These platforms provide greater transparency, faster approval times, and access to a broader range of financing options.

Actionable Steps for Leveraging Financing:

1. **Understand Your Debt-to-Income Ratio:** Ensure that your debt obligations are manageable in relation to your income to avoid overleveraging.
2. **Choose the Right Financing Option:** Select a financing method that aligns with your investment strategy, risk tolerance, and market conditions.
3. **Negotiate Loan Terms:** Work with lenders to secure favorable interest rates and repayment terms. Always aim to structure deals that protect your cash flow.
4. **Explore Creative Financing Solutions:** Look beyond traditional bank loans to explore options like seller financing, syndication, and partnerships to maximize your resources.

The SMILE Philosophy and Financing

The SMILE philosophy's focus on safety and inclusivity can be applied to financing strategies by ensuring that investments are responsibly leveraged and accessible to a diverse range of investors. Safety in financing means avoiding overleveraging and ensuring that debt is manageable. Inclusivity in financing involves creating opportunities for investors of all backgrounds to participate in real estate ventures through creative and flexible financing options.

By adopting financing strategies that align with the SMILE philosophy, real estate investors can build resilient portfolios while promoting financial accessibility and community growth. This approach not only enhances financial returns but also contributes to the overall well-being of the communities in which they invest.

Real estate investors often rely on financing to acquire properties and expand their portfolios. Understanding different financing options and their implications is crucial for managing debt and maximizing returns.

Example: Ken McElroy's Leverage Strategy

Ken McElroy, a prominent real estate investor and advisor to Robert Kiyosaki, advocates for the strategic use of leverage to grow a real estate portfolio. McElroy emphasizes that responsible borrowing can help investors acquire more properties and increase their returns, as long as the cash flow from the properties exceeds the cost of debt.

Actionable Steps for Leveraging Financing:

- **Understand Your Debt-to-Income Ratio:** Ensure that your debt obligations are manageable in relation to your income.
- **Choose the Right Financing Option:** Select a financing method that aligns with your investment strategy and risk tolerance.
- **Negotiate Loan Terms:** Work with lenders to secure favorable interest rates and repayment terms.

Tax Strategies for Real Estate Investors

Tax planning is a critical component of financial strategy in real estate investing. Investors who optimize their tax strategies can significantly reduce their tax liabilities and increase their net returns. Understanding the nuances of tax laws, deductions, and credits can provide real estate investors with a substantial financial advantage.

Example: David Bach's Pay Yourself First Philosophy

David Bach, author of *The Automatic Millionaire*, emphasizes the importance of tax-advantaged accounts and strategies to build wealth. Real estate investors can apply this principle by taking advantage of tax deductions, depreciation, and tax-deferred exchanges. Bach's philosophy of "paying yourself first" extends to ensuring that investors maximize their after-tax returns by leveraging available tax benefits.

Example: Tom Wheelwright's Tax Strategy Insights

Tom Wheelwright, a renowned tax advisor and author of *Tax-Free Wealth*, emphasizes that the tax code is designed to incentivize certain behaviors, including real estate investing. He advises investors to view the tax code as a guide to reducing taxes legally by aligning investments with government incentives. For instance, taking advantage of deductions for depreciation, energy-efficient upgrades, and property improvements can significantly lower taxable income.

Example: Anderson Tax and Business Advisors' Approach to Asset Protection and Tax Efficiency

Anderson Tax and Business Advisors advocate for a holistic approach to tax planning that goes beyond simple deductions. They emphasize the importance of structuring real estate investments through legal entities such as LLCs to protect personal assets from liability and reduce tax liabilities. Their philosophy revolves around maximizing tax benefits while ensuring compliance with tax laws.

One of Anderson's key strategies involves utilizing cost segregation studies to accelerate depreciation, allowing investors to significantly reduce their taxable income. They also stress the importance of proactive tax planning, recommending that investors work closely with tax professionals to stay ahead of legislative changes and identify new tax-saving opportunities.

Key Tax Strategies for Real Estate Investors:

1. **Depreciation:** One of the most powerful tax advantages in real estate, depreciation allows investors to deduct a portion of the property's value each year to account for wear and tear. This non-cash expense can offset rental income and reduce taxable income.
2. **1031 Exchange:** The 1031 exchange allows investors to defer capital gains taxes when selling a property, provided the proceeds are reinvested in a similar property. This strategy enables investors to grow their portfolios tax-deferred, preserving more capital for future investments.
3. **Real Estate Professional Status:** Investors who qualify as real estate professionals can unlock additional tax benefits, including the ability to deduct passive losses from active income. Meeting the requirements for this status can significantly reduce overall tax liability.
4. **Property Tax Appeals:** Regularly reviewing and appealing property tax assessments can ensure that investors are not overpaying property taxes. This can be particularly important in areas where property values have fluctuated significantly.

Example: Robert Kiyosaki's Use of Tax Strategies

Robert Kiyosaki, author of *Rich Dad Poor Dad*, highlights the importance of understanding tax laws to build wealth through real estate. Kiyosaki stresses that tax benefits, such as depreciation and 1031 exchanges, are critical tools that investors must leverage to maximize their returns and minimize tax liabilities.

Actionable Steps for Tax Planning:

1. **Consult a Tax Professional:** Work with a CPA or tax advisor who specializes in real estate. A knowledgeable advisor can help you identify tax-saving opportunities and ensure compliance with tax laws.
2. **Keep Detailed Records:** Maintain accurate records of all income, expenses, and property improvements. Proper documentation is essential for claiming deductions and avoiding issues during tax audits.
3. **Stay Informed on Tax Law Changes:** Tax laws are subject to change, and staying informed can help investors adapt their strategies to maximize tax benefits. Regular consultations with a tax professional can keep investors updated on new opportunities and requirements.
4. **Incorporate Energy-Efficient Upgrades:** Many governments offer tax incentives for energy-efficient property improvements. Installing solar panels, upgrading insulation, or replacing old appliances can provide both immediate and long-term tax benefits.

Example: Grant Cardone's Approach to Tax Efficiency

Grant Cardone, a real estate mogul known for his aggressive investment strategies, emphasizes the importance of tax efficiency in real estate investing. Cardone leverages cost segregation studies to accelerate depreciation deductions and reduce his taxable income. He also uses 1031 exchanges to defer capital gains taxes and reinvest profits into larger properties.

The Role of Technology in Tax Planning

Technology has revolutionized tax planning for real estate investors. Software solutions such as QuickBooks, Stessa, and TaxBot help investors track expenses, generate reports, and identify tax-saving opportunities. Additionally, platforms like Cost Segregation Services provide specialized tools to help investors accelerate depreciation deductions and reduce tax liabilities.

The SMILE Philosophy and Tax Strategies

The SMILE philosophy emphasizes morality and inclusivity, both of which are integral to responsible tax planning. By adhering to ethical tax practices, investors can ensure compliance with laws while maximizing their financial outcomes. Inclusivity can be promoted by using tax savings to invest in affordable housing projects or community initiatives, thereby creating positive social impacts.

By aligning their tax strategies with the SMILE philosophy, real estate investors can achieve both financial success and social responsibility. Tax planning is not merely about reducing liabilities but also about reinvesting savings into projects that benefit communities and create long-term value.

Tax Strategies Are Vital

Tax strategies are a vital component of sustainable real estate investing. By understanding and implementing tax planning techniques, investors can significantly enhance their financial returns while contributing to positive community impact. Learning from industry leaders like David Bach, Tom Wheelwright, Robert Kiyosaki, Grant Cardone, and Anderson Tax and Business Advisors, investors can develop tax strategies that align with the SMILE philosophy and promote long-term success.

Tax planning is a critical component of financial strategy in real estate investing. Investors who optimize their tax strategies can significantly reduce their tax liabilities and increase their net returns. Understanding the nuances of tax laws, deductions, and credits can provide real estate investors with a substantial financial advantage.

Building a Resilient Portfolio

Diversification is a key strategy for managing risk and ensuring the sustainability of a real estate portfolio. By investing in different property types and geographic locations, investors can reduce their exposure to market-specific risks. Building a resilient portfolio requires balancing cash flow, leveraging financing, and strategically acquiring properties that withstand market fluctuations.

Example: Sam Zell's Diversification Approach

Sam Zell, one of the most successful real estate investors, is known for his diversified portfolio, which includes multifamily properties, office buildings, industrial spaces, and retail centers. Zell's approach demonstrates the importance of spreading investments across various asset classes to achieve long-term stability. He emphasizes that a diversified portfolio can weather economic downturns more effectively, reducing overall risk.

Barbara Corcoran's Focus on Regional Diversification

Barbara Corcoran, founder of The Corcoran Group, stresses the importance of geographic diversification. She advises investors to explore different regions and markets to mitigate localized risks. For instance, an investor with properties in multiple states is less vulnerable to economic downturns or regulatory changes in a single location. Corcoran's philosophy encourages investors to stay adaptable and seize opportunities in emerging markets.

David Lindahl's Emerging Market Strategy

David Lindahl, a seasoned real estate investor, focuses on identifying emerging markets before they peak. He emphasizes the importance of investing in markets with strong job growth, population increases, and favorable economic conditions. Lindahl's strategy involves targeting markets in the early stages of growth, allowing investors to benefit from appreciation and long-term stability. His approach aligns with building a resilient portfolio by ensuring that properties remain valuable and profitable over time.

Ken McElroy's Approach to Asset Classes

Ken McElroy, a real estate advisor to Robert Kiyosaki, highlights the importance of investing in various asset classes. He advocates for including multifamily properties, commercial spaces, and storage units in a portfolio to balance risk and maximize returns. McElroy emphasizes that each asset class responds differently to economic changes, and diversification helps investors maintain consistent cash flow.

Grant Cardone's Syndication Model

Grant Cardone leverages syndication to build resilient portfolios by pooling resources from multiple investors to acquire large-scale properties. This approach reduces individual risk while allowing investors to participate in high-value deals. Cardone's model demonstrates how collaboration and shared investments can strengthen a portfolio's resilience and reduce exposure to market volatility.

Actionable Steps for Diversifying Your Portfolio:

1. **Invest in Different Property Types:** Diversifying across various property types—such as residential, commercial, industrial, and mixed-use properties—can help reduce risk. Each property type reacts differently to economic changes, ensuring a balanced portfolio. For instance, during an economic downturn, industrial properties might remain stable due to the demand for warehousing and logistics, while commercial office spaces might see a decline. By spreading investments across these types, investors can mitigate the impact of market fluctuations.
2. **Expand Geographically:** Investing in different regions and markets helps to minimize location-specific risks, such as natural disasters, regulatory changes, or localized economic downturns. For example, an investor with properties in both urban centers and suburban areas can benefit from different demand patterns. As seen during the COVID-19 pandemic, suburban properties saw increased demand due to remote work trends, while urban office spaces faced challenges. Geographic diversification ensures that an investor's portfolio remains resilient regardless of regional economic changes.
3. **Explore Alternative Investments:** Beyond traditional property acquisitions, consider alternative investments such as real estate investment trusts (REITs), crowdfunding platforms, and real estate syndications. These options allow investors to participate in larger deals with lower capital requirements and spread risk across multiple properties. For instance, REITs provide exposure to diversified property portfolios, including commercial, residential, and healthcare properties, without the need for direct property management. Crowdfunding platforms

offer opportunities to invest in niche markets or specialized projects, further diversifying the portfolio.

4. **Focus on Emerging Markets:** Identify markets with strong growth potential and invest early to capitalize on appreciation. Emerging markets often experience rapid increases in property values due to factors such as population growth, infrastructure development, and economic expansion. David Lindahl emphasizes the importance of targeting these markets before they peak, allowing investors to benefit from both cash flow and appreciation. By monitoring job growth, demographic shifts, and local government initiatives, investors can identify areas with significant upside potential. Investing in emerging markets not only diversifies a portfolio but also positions investors for substantial long-term gains. For example, cities like Austin, Texas, and Nashville, Tennessee, have become emerging market hotspots due to their thriving tech industries and growing populations. Real estate investors who recognized these trends early on were able to acquire properties at lower prices and benefit from rapid appreciation. Identify markets with strong growth potential and invest early to capitalize on appreciation.
5. **Leverage Technology:** Use data analytics and market research tools to identify diversification opportunities and track portfolio performance. Technology platforms like Roofstock, Fundrise, and RealtyMogul provide investors with insights into market trends, property performance, and investment opportunities. These platforms allow investors to remotely manage properties, analyze potential markets, and make data-driven decisions to enhance portfolio resilience.
6. Smart home technologies and IoT devices can also improve property management, reduce operating costs, and enhance tenant experiences. For example, integrating smart locks, thermostats, and security systems can streamline property operations and reduce vacancy rates by attracting tech-savvy tenants.
7. Additionally, blockchain technology is revolutionizing real estate transactions by providing greater transparency and security. Blockchain-based platforms like Propy enable investors to conduct transactions with reduced risk of fraud

and lower administrative costs. Embracing technology not only improves operational efficiency but also provides a competitive edge in identifying and capitalizing on new investment opportunities. Use data analytics and market research tools to identify diversification opportunities and track portfolio performance.

Technology's Role in Building Resilient Portfolios

Technology plays a crucial role in helping investors build resilient portfolios. Platforms such as Roofstock and Fundrise provide tools to identify new markets, track property performance, and manage investments remotely. Data analytics can help investors forecast market trends and make informed decisions about where to invest next.

The SMILE Philosophy and Building Resilient Portfolios

The SMILE philosophy emphasizes safety, inclusivity, and experiential learning, all of which are essential for building resilient portfolios. By diversifying investments, maintaining financial safeguards, and continuously learning about market trends, investors can ensure that their portfolios remain stable and profitable in various economic conditions. Inclusivity involves ensuring that properties serve diverse community needs, while safety focuses on minimizing risk through diversification.

A Resilient Portfolio is Essential

Building a resilient portfolio is essential for long-term success in real estate investing. By diversifying across property types, geographic locations, and asset classes, investors can reduce risk and enhance financial stability. Drawing inspiration from industry leaders like Sam Zell, Barbara Corcoran, David Lindahl, Ken McElroy, and Grant Cardone, investors can adopt strategies that align with the SMILE philosophy to promote sustainable growth and positive community impact. A resilient portfolio not only provides consistent returns but also supports long-term wealth creation and community development.

Diversification is a key strategy for managing risk and ensuring the sustainability of a real estate portfolio. By investing in different property types and geographic locations, investors can reduce their exposure to market-specific risks.

Example: Sam Zell's Diversification Approach

Sam Zell, one of the most successful real estate investors, is known for his diversified portfolio, which includes multifamily properties, office buildings, industrial spaces, and retail centers. Zell's approach demonstrates the importance of spreading investments across various asset classes to achieve long-term stability.

Actionable Steps for Diversifying Your Portfolio:

- **Invest in Different Property Types:** Consider residential, commercial, industrial, and mixed-use properties.
- **Expand Geographically:** Invest in properties across different regions to reduce exposure to local market fluctuations.
- **Explore Alternative Investments:** Consider investments in real estate investment trusts (REITs), crowdfunding platforms, or real estate syndications.

The SMILE Philosophy and Financial Strategies

The SMILE philosophy's focus on safety, morality, inclusivity, linguistic clarity, and experiential learning aligns with sustainable financial strategies in real estate investing. By adopting responsible financial practices, investors can create positive social impact while achieving financial success.

Safety: Financial safeguards, such as maintaining reserve funds and optimizing cash flow, ensure that investors can navigate economic downturns.

Morality: Ethical financing and tax planning practices promote transparency and integrity in real estate transactions.

Inclusivity: Providing affordable housing options and engaging with diverse communities contributes to social equity.

Linguistic Clarity: Clear communication with tenants, lenders, and partners builds trust and fosters long-term relationships.

Experiential Learning: Continuously improving financial literacy and staying informed about market trends ensures that investors make informed decisions.

Conclusion

Financial strategies are the foundation of sustainable real estate growth. By managing cash flow, leveraging financing options, optimizing tax strategies, and diversifying their portfolios, investors can achieve long-term stability and success. The insights from industry leaders such as Robert Kiyosaki, David Lindahl, Ken McElroy, David Bach, Sam Zell, and Grant Cardone provide valuable guidance for navigating the financial aspects of real estate investing.

Aligning financial strategies with the SMILE philosophy ensures that real estate investments are not only profitable but also ethical and community focused. By adopting responsible financial practices, investors can create lasting value and make meaningful contributions to the communities they serve. The SMILE philosophy emphasizes that financial success should not come at the expense of social responsibility. Instead, investors are encouraged to balance profitability with community impact, creating developments that benefit both investors and society.

In an ever-changing real estate landscape, the ability to adapt and innovate is crucial. Leveraging technology, staying informed about market trends, and maintaining a long-term vision are essential for building resilient portfolios. The combination of ethical practices and sound financial strategies creates a framework that ensures investments remain viable and impactful for years to come.

Real estate investors who prioritize sustainability and community engagement will be better positioned to navigate economic fluctuations and capitalize on emerging opportunities. By following the financial strategies outlined in this chapter and integrating them with the principles of the SMILE philosophy, investors can achieve financial independence while making a positive difference in their communities.

Ultimately, successful real estate investing is about more than just generating returns—it's about creating lasting, meaningful value. Through a commitment to ethical investing, continuous learning, and strategic planning, investors can ensure that their financial success contributes to a better future for everyone involved.

Chapter 6
Leveraging Technology in Real Estate

The Rise of PropTech

The real estate industry is undergoing a significant transformation, driven by technological advancements collectively known as PropTech. These innovations are reshaping property management, investment strategies, and tenant experiences. Key trends include the integration of Artificial Intelligence (AI), the Internet of Things (IoT), Virtual Reality (VR), and blockchain technology.

Artificial Intelligence (AI):

AI is enhancing property valuations, predictive maintenance, and tenant interactions. For instance, AI-driven analytics provide investors with actionable insights into market trends and tenant behaviors, enabling informed decision-making. Companies like Zillow and Redfin utilize AI to offer real-time data insights, helping investors stay ahead of market trends and adjust their strategies accordingly.

Advancements in AI Applications

Recent advancements in AI have introduced tools capable of automating tenant screening processes, reducing property management overhead, and improving the accuracy of property valuations. AI-powered chatbots are now being used to handle tenant inquiries, schedule property showings, and manage maintenance requests, significantly enhancing the tenant experience while reducing workload for property managers.

Example: Leveraging Predictive AI

Predictive AI tools help investors anticipate market changes and optimize rental pricing strategies. For instance, AI-driven platforms like HouseCanary and Reonomy use vast datasets to provide investors with market forecasts, helping them make data-driven decisions. These tools can predict neighborhood appreciation rates, tenant behaviors, and property performance metrics, which are invaluable for long-term planning.

Example: Blackstone's Use of AI in Asset Management

Blackstone, one of the world's largest real estate investment firms, has integrated AI to optimize its asset management practices. By leveraging AI, Blackstone can analyze tenant data, track property performance, and identify areas for cost savings and revenue growth. Their AI-driven approach has enhanced operational efficiency and allowed them to scale their portfolio effectively.

AI and the SMILE Philosophy

AI aligns with the SMILE philosophy by promoting safety through enhanced security features, ensuring inclusivity by reducing human biases in tenant screening, and fostering experiential learning by providing real-time data insights. By adopting AI, investors can make ethical, informed decisions that benefit both their portfolios and the communities they serve. AI is enhancing property valuations, predictive maintenance, and tenant interactions. For instance, AI-driven analytics provide investors with actionable insights into market trends and tenant behaviors, enabling informed decision-making. Companies like Zillow and Redfin utilize AI to offer real-time data insights, helping investors stay ahead of market trends and adjust their strategies accordingly.

Internet of Things (IoT):

IoT devices, such as smart thermostats, lighting systems, and security solutions, are becoming standard in properties, improving tenant satisfaction and property values. These technologies optimize energy consumption, enhance security, and contribute to more efficient property management. Companies like Nest and Ring have made IoT solutions more accessible, benefiting both property managers and tenants.

Expansion of IoT in Commercial Real Estate

The adoption of IoT extends beyond residential properties into commercial real estate (CRE). Smart office buildings now feature IoT-enabled lighting, HVAC systems, and occupancy sensors that reduce energy consumption and enhance productivity. These innovations create healthier work environments by monitoring air quality, temperature, and lighting conditions in real-time.

Example: Smart Building Systems in Action

For example, the Edge in Amsterdam, one of the world's smartest buildings, leverages IoT to optimize everything from lighting to workspace allocation. The building uses a network of sensors to adjust settings based on occupancy, maximizing energy efficiency and creating a comfortable working environment for its tenants. This approach has set a benchmark for sustainable and tech-enabled buildings worldwide.

Example: Ken McElroy's Use of IoT for Property Management

Ken McElroy, a seasoned property manager and real estate investor, integrates IoT devices in his properties to streamline operations and reduce costs. Smart sensors help McElroy monitor water usage, detect leaks, and manage energy consumption across his portfolio, leading to substantial savings and more efficient property management.

Enhancing Tenant Experience with IoT

IoT devices also enhance the tenant experience by offering convenience and customization. Smart locks, for instance, allow tenants to control access remotely, improving security and flexibility. Voice-activated assistants can manage lighting and temperature settings, making everyday tasks more convenient.

Example: Grant Cardone's Focus on Smart Amenities

Grant Cardone incorporates IoT-based smart amenities into his multifamily properties to attract tech-savvy tenants. His properties feature smart home systems that allow tenants to control their living environment through mobile apps, improving tenant satisfaction and retention rates.

IoT and the SMILE Philosophy

The integration of IoT aligns with the SMILE philosophy by promoting safety and inclusivity. Smart devices improve security and reduce operational risks, ensuring safer living and working environments. Additionally, by making technology more accessible, IoT fosters inclusivity, ensuring that tech-driven solutions benefit a wide range of tenants. IoT devices, such as smart thermostats and security systems, are becoming standard in properties, improving tenant satisfaction and property values. These technologies optimize energy consumption and enhance security, contributing to more efficient property management. Companies like Nest and Ring have made IoT solutions more accessible, benefiting both property managers and tenants.

Virtual Reality (VR):

VR tours allow potential tenants to explore properties remotely, providing a convenient, immersive experience that saves time for both tenants and property managers. This technology became especially valuable during the COVID-19 pandemic when in-person showings were limited. VR tools continue to grow in popularity, especially in competitive rental markets.

Expanding Use Cases for VR in Real Estate

Beyond virtual tours, VR is now being used to visualize renovation projects and new developments before they are completed. Investors and developers can create immersive experiences that showcase properties in their future state, helping potential buyers and tenants envision the final product. This capability can be particularly useful in off-plan sales, where properties are marketed before construction is finished.

Example: VR in Commercial Leasing

In the commercial real estate sector, VR is being used to help businesses design their office spaces. Tenants can use VR tools to customize layouts, furniture arrangements, and decor before signing a lease. This reduces the time and cost associated with physical modifications and ensures that tenants move into spaces that meet their exact specifications.

Example: Barbara Corcoran's Advocacy for VR

Barbara Corcoran, founder of The Corcoran Group, has been a strong advocate for using VR to enhance the buying and renting experience. She believes that VR can help real estate professionals stand out in a crowded market by providing clients with a more engaging and informative experience. Corcoran also emphasizes that VR can make properties more accessible to a global audience, increasing the potential pool of buyers and tenants.

VR and the SMILE Philosophy

Virtual reality aligns with the SMILE philosophy by promoting inclusivity and experiential learning. By offering immersive tours, VR makes properties more accessible to people who may not be able to visit in person due to geographical or mobility constraints. This fosters inclusivity by ensuring that everyone, regardless of location or physical ability, can explore potential homes or investment opportunities. Additionally, VR enhances experiential learning by allowing investors to visualize potential changes and upgrades, making more informed decisions about property investments. VR tours allow potential tenants to explore properties remotely, providing a convenient, immersive experience that saves time for both tenants and property managers. This technology became especially valuable during the COVID-19 pandemic when in-person showings were limited. VR tools continue to grow in popularity, especially in competitive rental markets.

Blockchain Technology:

Blockchain technology is revolutionizing real estate transactions by providing secure, transparent, and tamper-proof records. This technology reduces the risk of fraud and streamlines the buying and selling process. Blockchain offers an immutable ledger system that ensures all transaction details are recorded accurately and cannot be altered, providing peace of mind to both buyers and sellers.

Expanding Use Cases for Blockchain in Real Estate

Beyond secure transactions, blockchain is also being used to streamline property management processes, tokenization of real estate assets, and smart contracts. Tokenization allows investors to purchase fractional ownership of properties through digital tokens, opening up real estate investing to a broader audience. This democratization of property ownership can create more inclusive investment opportunities.

Example: Tokenized Real Estate Investments

Platforms like RealtyBits and RealT have pioneered the concept of tokenized real estate investments. These platforms enable investors to buy shares in properties using blockchain-based tokens, making it easier for individuals to diversify their real estate portfolios with lower capital requirements. Tokenization increases liquidity in the real estate market by allowing fractional ownership and enabling faster transactions.

Example: Smart Contracts in Property Transactions

Smart contracts, powered by blockchain, automate various aspects of property transactions, reducing the need for intermediaries. For instance, once predefined conditions are met, such as the completion of inspections or receipt of payments, the smart contract automatically executes the next steps in the process. This reduces administrative tasks and speeds up transactions.

Example: Propy's Blockchain Platform

Propy, a blockchain-based real estate platform, facilitates secure property transactions using blockchain technology. This innovation ensures that all parties involved in a transaction have access to verified, immutable records, reducing the risk of disputes and improving transparency. Propy has successfully executed blockchain-based property sales, proving the feasibility of this technology in real-world applications.

Blockchain and the SMILE Philosophy

Blockchain aligns with the SMILE philosophy by promoting safety, morality, and inclusivity. The transparency and security offered by blockchain technology ensure that real estate transactions are conducted ethically and fairly. By reducing the risk of fraud and increasing accessibility through tokenization, blockchain promotes inclusivity in real estate investing. Additionally, the use of smart contracts enhances linguistic clarity by reducing the complexity of legal documents and ensuring that all parties understand the terms of the agreement.

The Future of Blockchain in Real Estate

As blockchain technology continues to evolve, its applications in real estate are expected to grow. From secure property transactions to innovative investment models, blockchain will play a pivotal role in transforming the industry. Investors who embrace blockchain technology early will be well-positioned to take advantage of these advancements and create more resilient, future-proof portfolios. Blockchain provides secure, transparent, and tamper-proof records, reducing the risk of fraud and streamlining property transactions. Platforms like Propy facilitate secure property transactions using blockchain technology, ensuring that all parties involved have access to verified, immutable records. Blockchain's use in real estate is expected to grow, making transactions more efficient and trustworthy.

Embracing these PropTech innovations enables real estate professionals to enhance operational efficiency, improve tenant experiences, and stay competitive in an evolving market landscape. By adopting technologies such as AI, IoT, VR, and blockchain, investors can create more resilient portfolios that are better equipped to handle future challenges.

Technology is reshaping the real estate industry, creating opportunities for investors to improve efficiency, enhance tenant experiences, and future-proof their portfolios. The rise of property technology (PropTech) has introduced innovative solutions for property management, market analysis, and tenant engagement.

Example: Smart Building Technologies

Smart building technologies, such as automated lighting, temperature control, and security systems, are becoming increasingly popular. These technologies not only improve tenant comfort and safety but also reduce operational costs. Companies like Nest and Ring have revolutionized home security and automation, making smart features more accessible to property owners and tenants.

Example: Zillow and Redfin's Data-Driven Approaches

Platforms like Zillow and Redfin have transformed how properties are bought and sold by leveraging big data and AI. These platforms provide real-time market insights, enabling investors to make informed decisions. By integrating data-driven tools into their investment strategies, real estate professionals can identify trends, predict market shifts, and optimize property performance.

Enhancing Tenant Experience with Technology

One of the most impactful applications of technology in real estate is improving tenant experiences. From virtual tours to smart home integrations, technology makes it easier for tenants to find, secure, and enjoy their living spaces. Tenants expect more from their living environments today, and technology provides solutions that cater to these evolving demands.

Personalized Living Experiences

AI and IoT devices are now being used to create personalized living experiences. Smart home systems can learn tenant preferences for lighting, temperature, and security, adjusting automatically to meet individual needs. This personalization enhances tenant satisfaction and contributes to higher retention rates.

Expanding Personalization with AI

Advanced AI algorithms are enabling even more customization for tenants. For example, AI systems can now predict a tenant's daily routines and adjust home settings accordingly. These systems can recognize when a tenant typically returns home from work and ensure the home is at their preferred temperature and lighting level upon arrival. This level of personalization not only enhances comfort but also improves energy efficiency, benefiting both tenants and property owners.

Example: Customized Services in Smart Apartments

Several smart apartment communities now offer residents the ability to customize their living experiences through mobile apps. Tenants can schedule maintenance, book community amenities, and receive personalized recommendations for local services. This seamless integration of technology into everyday life fosters a sense of belonging and satisfaction among tenants.

Health and Wellness Enhancements

Personalized living spaces are also incorporating health and wellness features. Smart air purifiers, humidity monitors, and fitness tracking integrations are becoming standard in luxury apartments. These features cater to health-conscious tenants, creating an environment that promotes overall well-being.

Example: Smart Wellness Communities

Developments such as Delos Living have pioneered the concept of wellness-focused communities. These properties integrate personalized wellness features, including air and water purification systems and circadian lighting, which adjusts throughout the day to support natural sleep patterns. This approach demonstrates how personalization can go beyond convenience to improve quality of life.

Personalization and the SMILE Philosophy

Personalized living spaces align with the SMILE philosophy by promoting safety and inclusivity. Smart systems ensure homes are safe and accessible for all residents, regardless of their physical abilities. Personalized features also support experiential learning by providing tenants with tools to better understand and manage their living environments, fostering a more engaged and informed community.

AI and IoT devices are now being used to create personalized living experiences. Smart home systems can learn tenant preferences for lighting, temperature, and security, adjusting automatically to meet individual needs. This personalization enhances tenant satisfaction and contributes to higher retention rates.

Example: Smart Home Automation

Smart home automation systems like Google Nest and Amazon Alexa have transformed tenant experiences by offering seamless control over various home features. Tenants can control lighting, heating, and security through voice commands or mobile apps, creating a more convenient and enjoyable living environment.

Tenant Portals for Seamless Communication

Tenant portals are another way technology is enhancing the tenant experience. These platforms allow tenants to pay rent, submit maintenance requests, and communicate with property managers in real-time. By improving communication, these portals reduce misunderstandings and foster positive relationships between tenants and property managers.

Expanding Tenant Portal Features

Modern tenant portals are evolving to offer a broader range of features that enhance tenant engagement and satisfaction. In addition to rent payments and maintenance requests, many portals now include community forums, event calendars, and personalized notifications.

These features create a sense of community within the property and keep tenants informed about updates, events, and important announcements.

Example: AppFolio's Tenant Portal

AppFolio's tenant portal offers a comprehensive solution for property management communication. Tenants can view their payment history, sign lease agreements electronically, and even schedule maintenance appointments at their convenience. The platform also includes a messaging system that allows tenants and property managers to communicate directly, improving transparency and reducing response times.

Security and Privacy Enhancements

With increasing concerns about data security, tenant portals are incorporating advanced security measures to protect sensitive information. Features such as two-factor authentication, encrypted communications, and secure document storage ensure that tenant data remains safe and private. These security enhancements build trust between tenants and property managers.

Example: Building Trust with Secure Portals

Secure portals, like those offered by Buildium and Yardi, emphasize privacy and data protection. By prioritizing security, these platforms create a trustworthy environment that encourages tenants to engage more actively with property management.

Tenant Portals and the SMILE Philosophy

Tenant portals align with the SMILE philosophy by promoting safety, linguistic clarity, and inclusivity. The secure and transparent communication channels provided by tenant portals ensure that tenants feel safe and well-informed. Linguistic clarity is achieved through clear messaging systems and easy-to-understand user interfaces. Additionally, portals that offer multilingual support promote inclusivity by accommodating tenants from diverse backgrounds. By enhancing tenant experiences through seamless communication, property managers can foster stronger relationships and achieve long-term tenant satisfaction.

Tenant portals are another way technology is enhancing the tenant experience. These platforms allow tenants to pay rent, submit maintenance requests, and communicate with property managers in real-time. By improving communication, these portals reduce misunderstandings and foster positive relationships between tenants and property managers.

Example: Buildium's Tenant Portal

Buildium offers a tenant portal that streamlines communication and administrative processes. Tenants can access their lease agreements, track maintenance requests, and receive updates from property managers, improving overall satisfaction and engagement.

Using AR for Interior Design

Augmented Reality (AR) tools are increasingly being used to help tenants visualize furniture placement and interior design options. Apps like IKEA Place allow users to see how furniture will look and fit in their space before making a purchase. This feature can be integrated into rental listings to enhance the tenant experience.

Expanding AR Applications in Real Estate

Beyond furniture placement, AR is now being used to assist property managers and developers in showcasing renovation plans and structural changes. Tenants can view potential upgrades or modifications to their living spaces before any physical changes are made. This capability reduces uncertainty and increases tenant confidence in property improvements.

Example: AR for Renovation Planning

AR tools like Houzz and Matterport offer solutions for renovation planning, enabling tenants and property owners to visualize new layouts, materials, and finishes in real-time. For example, a tenant considering a kitchen renovation can use AR to see how different cabinet styles, countertops, and appliances will look, helping them make informed decisions.

Example: Virtual Staging with AR

Virtual staging through AR is another growing trend in real estate. Companies like RoOomy and VirtualStagingLab use AR to stage vacant properties, making them more appealing to prospective tenants. This technology allows tenants to envision a furnished space, which has been shown to increase rental inquiries and reduce time on the market.

AR and the SMILE Philosophy

AR technology aligns with the SMILE philosophy by promoting experiential learning and inclusivity. By providing tenants with tools to visualize their living spaces, AR enhances decision-making and reduces the risk of dissatisfaction with property changes. Additionally, AR makes properties more accessible by allowing remote visualization, benefiting prospective tenants who may not be able to visit properties in person.

Augmented Reality (AR) tools are increasingly being used to help tenants visualize furniture placement and interior design options. Apps like IKEA Place allow users to see how furniture will look and fit in their space before making a purchase. This feature can be integrated into rental listings to enhance the tenant experience.

Example: Barbara Corcoran's Emphasis on Tenant Experience

Barbara Corcoran has often highlighted the importance of tenant satisfaction in real estate success. She advocates for using technology to improve tenant experiences, noting that happy tenants are more likely to renew leases and recommend properties to others.

Enhancing Inclusivity through Technology

Technology also promotes inclusivity by making properties more accessible to tenants with disabilities. Voice-activated assistants, for example, can help tenants with mobility challenges control their environment more easily. Additionally, virtual tours make properties accessible to prospective tenants who may not be able to visit in person due to geographical or physical limitations.

Expanding Digital Accessibility

Digital accessibility tools are being integrated into tenant portals and property management systems to accommodate users with different needs. Features such as text-to-speech functionality, screen readers, and customizable font sizes ensure that all tenants can navigate digital interfaces comfortably. This level of inclusivity broadens the range of potential tenants and creates a welcoming environment for all.

Example: Multilingual Support in Tenant Portals

Multilingual support in tenant portals allows property managers to communicate effectively with tenants from diverse backgrounds. Platforms like AppFolio and Buildium offer translation services that ensure tenants receive important information in their preferred language, reducing misunderstandings and fostering better relationships.

IoT Devices for Inclusive Living

IoT devices are also being used to create more inclusive living environments. Smart home systems can be tailored to meet the needs of individuals with disabilities, such as controlling lights, doors, and appliances through voice commands or mobile apps. These systems enhance independence and improve quality of life for tenants with special needs.

Example: Inclusive Design in Smart Apartments

Developers are increasingly incorporating inclusive design principles into smart apartments. For example, properties may include smart doorbells with video capabilities that provide visual alerts for hearing-impaired tenants or smart thermostats that adjust settings based on voice commands for tenants with mobility challenges.

Inclusivity and the SMILE Philosophy

Enhancing inclusivity through technology aligns perfectly with the SMILE philosophy by ensuring that everyone, regardless of their abilities or language preferences, can fully participate in their living environment. Providing accessible tools and communication channels fosters a sense of belonging and community, which is essential for long-term tenant satisfaction. Inclusivity not only benefits tenants but also enhances the reputation and appeal of property management companies, leading to stronger tenant retention rates and increased overall success.

Technology also promotes inclusivity by making properties more accessible to tenants with disabilities. Voice-activated assistants, for example, can help tenants with mobility challenges control their environment more easily. Additionally, virtual tours make properties accessible to prospective tenants who may not be able to visit in person due to geographical or physical limitations.

The SMILE Philosophy and Tenant Experience

Enhancing tenant experience aligns with the SMILE philosophy by fostering inclusivity, ensuring safety, and promoting continuous learning. Providing tenants with smart technologies and seamless communication tools creates a more secure and engaging living environment. By prioritizing tenant satisfaction, investors can achieve long-term success and build positive community relationships.

One of the most impactful applications of technology in real estate is improving tenant experiences. From virtual tours to smart home integrations, technology makes it easier for tenants to find, secure, and enjoy their living spaces.

Example: Virtual Reality Tours

Virtual reality (VR) tours allow potential tenants to explore properties remotely. This technology became especially valuable during the COVID-19 pandemic when in-person showings were limited. VR tours provide a convenient, immersive experience that saves time for both tenants and property managers.

Example: Grant Cardone's Use of Smart Tech

Grant Cardone, a well-known real estate investor, leverages smart technologies to enhance tenant satisfaction and reduce turnover. By integrating smart locks, thermostats, and security systems in his properties, Cardone ensures that his tenants have a modern, secure, and convenient living experience. This approach not only improves tenant retention but also increases property value.

Streamlining Property Management

Technology also streamlines property management processes, reducing administrative burdens and improving operational efficiency. Property management software solutions offer features such as rent collection, maintenance tracking, and tenant communication. These tools not only simplify routine tasks but also improve the overall tenant experience by ensuring faster response times and more transparent operations.

Example: Buildium and AppFolio

Platforms like Buildium and AppFolio provide comprehensive property management solutions, including features such as online rent payments, automated lease tracking, maintenance request management, and tenant screening. These platforms also offer mobile apps that enable property managers and tenants to stay connected, streamline communication, and handle administrative tasks efficiently. These tools automate tasks such as rent collection, lease management, and maintenance requests, allowing property managers to focus on strategic tasks rather than administrative ones. These platforms also offer mobile apps, enabling tenants to make payments, request repairs, and communicate with property managers on the go.

Emerging Technologies in Property Management

The use of emerging technologies like AI, IoT, and blockchain is further enhancing property management efficiency and effectiveness. These technologies are transforming how property managers handle daily operations, communicate with tenants, and maintain properties.

Example: AI-Powered Chatbots for Tenant Communication

AI-powered chatbots are becoming more common in property management, allowing tenants to get immediate responses to inquiries. Companies like RentCafe and PropertyVista have implemented AI-driven chatbots that can schedule maintenance requests, provide updates on rent payments, and answer frequently asked questions. For example, PropertyVista's chatbot, integrated into their tenant portal, has reduced response times and improved tenant satisfaction by automating routine queries and tasks. These chatbots can schedule maintenance requests, provide updates on rent payments, and answer frequently asked questions. By automating these tasks, property managers can focus on more complex issues, improving overall efficiency.

Example: Drones for Property Inspections

Drones are being used to conduct property inspections, particularly in large commercial properties. These devices can capture high-resolution images and videos of hard-to-reach areas, reducing the time and cost associated with traditional inspections. Drones are especially useful for inspecting roofs, facades, and large outdoor spaces, providing property managers with valuable data to address maintenance needs proactively.

Smart Sensors for Predictive Maintenance

Smart sensors are revolutionizing property maintenance by providing real-time data on building systems. These sensors can monitor HVAC systems, detect water leaks, and track energy usage. When abnormalities are detected, property managers receive alerts, allowing them to address issues before they escalate into costly repairs.

Expanding Capabilities of Smart Sensors

The latest smart sensors are capable of more than just monitoring building systems. They can now predict the lifespan of equipment, schedule maintenance automatically, and optimize energy consumption based on usage patterns. For example, smart lighting systems can adjust brightness levels depending on the time of day and occupancy, reducing energy costs and extending the lifespan of light fixtures.

Example: Preventing Water Damage with Smart Leak Detectors

Smart leak detectors are becoming a crucial tool for property managers. These devices can detect leaks early and send alerts to property managers, preventing significant water damage and reducing repair costs. Properties equipped with smart leak detectors have seen a substantial reduction in insurance claims related to water damage, making these sensors a valuable investment.

Predictive Maintenance and Cost Savings

Predictive maintenance using smart sensors can result in significant cost savings for property owners. By addressing maintenance issues proactively, property managers can avoid expensive emergency repairs and extend the lifespan of building systems. For example, a smart HVAC system can notify property managers when filters need to be replaced, reducing energy consumption and improving air quality.

Example: Smart Elevators in Commercial Buildings

Smart elevators equipped with sensors can monitor performance in real time and predict when maintenance is required. These systems reduce downtime and improve tenant satisfaction by ensuring that elevators remain operational. In high-rise buildings, smart elevators can optimize energy usage by adjusting to traffic patterns and reducing unnecessary stops.

Smart Sensors and the SMILE Philosophy

Smart sensors align with the SMILE philosophy by promoting safety, efficiency, and inclusivity. These devices enhance the safety of living and working environments by detecting potential risks early. They also promote efficiency by reducing energy consumption and maintenance costs. Inclusivity is achieved by ensuring that properties remain accessible and functional for all tenants, regardless of physical limitations, through proactive maintenance solutions.

Smart sensors are revolutionizing property maintenance by providing real-time data on building systems. These sensors can monitor HVAC systems, detect water leaks, and track energy usage. When abnormalities are detected, property managers receive alerts, allowing them to address issues before they escalate into costly repairs.

Example: Blockchain for Lease Agreements

Blockchain technology is being used to create secure, tamper-proof lease agreements. These digital contracts reduce the need for intermediaries, speed up the leasing process, and ensure that all terms are transparent and immutable. Blockchain-based lease agreements can also automate rent payments and renewals, further streamlining property management tasks.

Example: IoT-Integrated Security Systems

IoT-integrated security systems are providing enhanced safety for tenants. Smart locks, video surveillance, and access control systems can be managed remotely, allowing property managers to monitor and control security measures from anywhere. These systems also provide tenants with greater control over their personal safety, improving tenant satisfaction.

Emerging Technologies and the SMILE Philosophy

The integration of emerging technologies in property management aligns with the SMILE philosophy by promoting safety, inclusivity, and experiential learning. AI and IoT devices enhance safety by identifying potential risks and providing real-time solutions. Blockchain technology ensures transparent and ethical transactions, fostering trust between tenants and property managers. By adopting these innovations, property managers can create more efficient, inclusive, and secure living environments for their tenants.

The use of emerging technologies like AI and IoT is further enhancing property management efficiency. AI-driven chatbots, for instance, can handle tenant inquiries and maintenance requests automatically, freeing up property managers for more complex tasks. IoT devices, such as smart sensors, can monitor building systems in real time, detecting issues like water leaks or HVAC malfunctions before they become major problems.

Example: Leveraging IoT for Predictive Maintenance

Predictive maintenance, enabled by IoT, is becoming a game-changer in property management. By using sensors to monitor the condition of building systems, property managers can proactively address maintenance needs before they escalate. For example, smart HVAC systems can alert managers when filters need replacement or when energy usage is outside normal parameters, preventing costly breakdowns and reducing energy waste.

Example: Ken McElroy's Approach to Efficient Management

Ken McElroy, a seasoned real estate investor and property manager, emphasizes the importance of leveraging technology to improve property management efficiency. McElroy advises investors to adopt tools that streamline operations, enhance tenant communication, and provide actionable insights into property performance. His focus on data-driven management ensures that properties remain profitable and well-maintained.

Security Enhancements Through Technology

Technology also enhances security in property management. Digital key systems, smart locks, and video surveillance can be managed remotely, ensuring that properties remain secure without the need for on-site personnel. This reduces costs while improving tenant safety and satisfaction.

Expanding Security Measures

Advanced security technologies are now integrating facial recognition, biometric access controls, and AI-driven threat detection systems. These technologies allow property managers to identify potential security risks in real-time and respond proactively. Facial recognition systems, for example, can grant secure access to authorized individuals while denying entry to unauthorized persons, improving overall property safety.

Example: Biometric Access Controls

Biometric access control systems, such as fingerprint or retina scanners, provide an additional layer of security for tenants. These systems eliminate the need for traditional keys or access cards, reducing the risk of lost or stolen credentials. Biometric systems are now being implemented in high-end residential buildings and commercial properties to ensure only authorized individuals have access to secure areas.

Example: AI-Driven Threat Detection

AI-driven threat detection systems analyze security footage in real-time to identify suspicious behaviors or unauthorized access attempts. These systems can alert property managers to potential security breaches, allowing for swift responses. For example, if a camera detects someone loitering near an entrance, the system can automatically notify security personnel.

Smart Locks and Mobile Access

Smart locks with mobile access capabilities are becoming increasingly popular in residential and commercial properties. Tenants can unlock doors using their smartphones, eliminating the need for physical keys. Property managers can also grant temporary access to service providers or guests, improving convenience and security. Smart locks can be integrated with tenant portals to streamline access management.

Example: Video Surveillance with Remote Monitoring

Video surveillance systems equipped with remote monitoring capabilities allow property managers to keep an eye on their properties from anywhere. These systems can be accessed via mobile apps, providing real-time footage and alerts. Remote monitoring ensures that properties remain secure even when property managers are off-site.

Security Enhancements and the SMILE Philosophy

Security enhancements through technology align with the SMILE philosophy by promoting safety and inclusivity. Advanced security measures ensure that tenants feel safe and protected in their living environments. Additionally, mobile access solutions and biometric systems accommodate tenants with different needs, making properties more accessible and inclusive. By leveraging these technologies, property managers can foster trust and enhance tenant satisfaction while ensuring the long-term security of their properties.

Technology also enhances security in property management. Digital key systems, smart locks, and video surveillance can be managed remotely, ensuring that properties remain secure without the need for on-site personnel. This reduces costs while improving tenant safety and satisfaction.

Streamlining Operations and the SMILE Philosophy

Streamlining property management aligns with the SMILE philosophy by promoting safety, morality, and inclusivity. By ensuring that properties are well-maintained and secure, property managers create safer living environments for tenants. Transparent communication and proactive maintenance practices foster trust and positive relationships between tenants and property managers, promoting ethical management practices. Inclusivity is also enhanced by using digital tools that accommodate diverse tenant needs, including multilingual support and accessibility features.

Technology also streamlines property management processes, reducing administrative burdens and improving operational efficiency. Property management software solutions offer features such as rent collection, maintenance tracking, and tenant communication.

Data Analytics for Informed Decision-Making

Data analytics plays a crucial role in modern real estate investing. By analyzing market trends, tenant behaviors, and property performance, investors can make data-driven decisions to optimize their portfolios. Data analytics tools provide real-time insights that allow property managers to identify opportunities, reduce risks, and increase efficiency.

Example: Peter Linneman's Data-Driven Strategies

Peter Linneman, a leading real estate economist, has emphasized the importance of data analytics in his numerous publications and presentations, particularly focusing on its role in forecasting market trends and identifying investment opportunities. His work highlights that data-driven decision-making can significantly reduce risks and improve the success rate of real estate investments, as demonstrated in his seminal work, 'Real Estate Markets and Capital Markets.' Linneman stresses that data-driven decision-making reduces risks and increases the likelihood of success in real estate investing.

Example: Using Predictive Analytics

Predictive analytics tools can help investors anticipate market changes, adjust rental rates, and identify emerging markets. By leveraging these tools, investors can stay ahead of market trends and make proactive investment decisions.

Expanding Applications of Data Analytics

Beyond market trends, data analytics can be used to improve tenant retention and streamline operations. For example, property managers can analyze tenant feedback and behavior patterns to identify areas for improvement in property management. Understanding what tenants value most—whether it's quick maintenance responses or community amenities—can help managers tailor their services to meet tenant needs.

Example: Tenant Behavior Analytics

By analyzing tenant behavior data, property managers can predict which tenants are more likely to renew their leases. This insight allows managers to offer targeted incentives, such as rent discounts or lease renewal perks, to improve retention rates. Companies like RentSense use AI-driven analytics to help property managers reduce vacancies and optimize rental pricing.

Data Analytics for Maintenance Efficiency

Data analytics can also enhance maintenance efficiency by tracking the performance of building systems. For example, sensors can collect data on HVAC system performance, allowing property managers to schedule maintenance before issues arise. This predictive maintenance approach reduces downtime and lowers repair costs.

Example: Smart Building Analytics

Smart buildings equipped with IoT devices can provide detailed analytics on energy usage, occupancy patterns, and equipment performance. This data helps property managers optimize building operations, reduce costs, and improve tenant satisfaction. For instance, adjusting lighting and HVAC systems based on occupancy patterns can significantly reduce energy consumption.

The SMILE Philosophy and Data Analytics

Data analytics aligns with the SMILE philosophy by promoting experiential learning and informed decision-making. By continuously analyzing property performance and tenant feedback, property managers can learn from their experiences and make data-driven improvements. Additionally, data transparency fosters trust between property managers and tenants, promoting ethical and inclusive practices in real estate management.

Data analytics plays a crucial role in modern real estate investing. By analyzing market trends, tenant behaviors, and property performance, investors can make data-driven decisions to optimize their portfolios.

Blockchain for Transparent Transactions

Blockchain technology is revolutionizing real estate transactions by providing secure, transparent, and tamper-proof records. For example, in 2022, a $2.4 million property in Florida was sold entirely through a blockchain transaction facilitated by Propy, showcasing the potential of blockchain to simplify and secure real estate deals. Additionally, companies like Harbor have tokenized high-value commercial properties, enabling fractional ownership and increasing liquidity in traditionally illiquid markets. These real-world applications highlight blockchain's transformative impact on the real estate sector. This technology reduces the risk of fraud and streamlines the buying and selling process. Blockchain offers a decentralized ledger that ensures all transaction details are recorded accurately and cannot be altered, providing peace of mind to both buyers and sellers.

Example: Propy's Blockchain Platform

Propy, a blockchain-based real estate platform, facilitates secure property transactions using blockchain technology. This innovation ensures that all parties involved in a transaction have access to verified, immutable records, reducing the risk of disputes and improving transparency.

Example: Blackstone's Use of Blockchain for Property Sales

Blackstone, one of the world's largest real estate investment firms, has begun exploring blockchain technology to streamline property transactions. By using blockchain to automate title verification and reduce paperwork, Blackstone aims to reduce transaction times and costs while increasing security and transparency.

Example: RedSwan's Tokenization of Real Estate Assets

RedSwan, a commercial real estate tokenization platform, is utilizing blockchain to fractionalize ownership of high-value properties. This approach allows investors to buy shares in properties through digital tokens, making real estate investing more accessible. Tokenization enhances liquidity in the real estate market by allowing investors to trade their shares on blockchain marketplaces.

Example: Smart Contracts in Real Estate

Smart contracts, powered by blockchain, automate various aspects of property transactions. These digital contracts execute automatically when predefined conditions are met, such as the completion of inspections or receipt of payments. Smart contracts reduce the need for intermediaries, speeding up the transaction process and ensuring transparency.

Example: RealtyBits' Blockchain Platform

RealtyBits offers a blockchain platform that enables real estate investment funds to manage their portfolios more efficiently. By using blockchain for investor management, RealtyBits reduces administrative costs and ensures compliance with regulatory requirements. The platform also offers tokenized shares, making it easier for investors to diversify their holdings.

Blockchain and the SMILE Philosophy

Blockchain aligns with the SMILE philosophy by promoting safety, morality, and inclusivity. The transparency and security offered by blockchain technology ensure that real estate transactions are conducted ethically and fairly. By reducing the risk of fraud and increasing accessibility through tokenization, blockchain promotes inclusivity in real estate investing. Additionally, smart contracts provide linguistic clarity by reducing the complexity of legal documents and ensuring that all parties understand the terms of the agreement.

As blockchain technology continues to evolve, its applications in real estate are expected to grow. From secure property transactions to innovative investment models, blockchain will play a pivotal role in transforming the industry. Real estate investors who adopt blockchain early will be well-positioned to benefit from these advancements and create more secure, efficient, and inclusive portfolios.

Blockchain technology is revolutionizing real estate transactions by providing secure, transparent, and tamper-proof records. This technology reduces the risk of fraud and streamlines the buying and selling process.

The SMILE Philosophy and Technology Integration

The SMILE philosophy—Safety, Morality, Inclusivity, Linguistic Clarity, and Experiential Learning—serves as a guiding framework for integrating technology into real estate management. This philosophy, as articulated by SMILE Company LLC, emphasizes creating positive community impact and ethical business practices through the strategic use of technology. By fostering safer environments, promoting transparency, and enhancing accessibility, the SMILE framework ensures that technology adoption in real estate aligns with the broader goal of community-centric growth. This philosophy promotes ethical practices, transparent operations, and community-focused growth through the responsible use of technology.

1. **Safety:** Smart home technologies, such as smart locks, IoT-integrated security systems, and AI-driven threat detection, enhance tenant safety by providing real-time monitoring and automated responses to potential security breaches. These technologies ensure that tenants feel secure in their living environments, which is a core aspect of the SMILE philosophy.
2. **Morality:** Blockchain technology ensures secure, tamper-proof records of real estate transactions, reducing fraud and promoting ethical practices. Platforms like Propy and RealtyBits facilitate such transparent dealings. By implementing transparent processes, property managers and investors can ensure fairness and accountability in their operations.
3. **Inclusivity:** Digital platforms offer features that cater to diverse tenant needs, including multilingual support and accessibility options, ensuring equitable access to services. IoT devices and AI-driven tools can also make properties more accessible to individuals with disabilities, creating inclusive living environments that cater to a broader range of tenants.
4. **Linguistic Clarity:** Clear communication channels provided by AI-powered chatbots and tenant portals reduce misunderstandings and ensure that all parties have access to accurate information. Technology simplifies complex processes like lease agreements and payment structures, making them easier to understand for tenants from various backgrounds.

5. **Experiential Learning:** Leveraging data analytics allows property managers to learn from tenant behaviors and market trends, facilitating continuous improvement in services and operations. Real-time data insights enable managers to adapt their strategies and optimize performance, aligning with the experiential learning principle of the SMILE philosophy.

By embracing these technological solutions, real estate professionals can effectively implement the SMILE philosophy, leading to improved tenant satisfaction, operational efficiency, and ethical management practices. The integration of emerging technologies not only aligns with the core values of the SMILE philosophy but also ensures that real estate investments contribute positively to the communities they serve. The SMILE philosophy's focus on safety, morality, inclusivity, linguistic clarity, and experiential learning aligns perfectly with the integration of technology in real estate.

Chapter 7
Building and Managing a Diversified Portfolio

Diversifying a real estate portfolio is essential for reducing risk and increasing long-term profitability. By spreading investments across various property types, locations, and market segments, investors can create a resilient portfolio capable of weathering economic shifts and market volatility. This chapter explores the principles of diversification, practical strategies for portfolio management, and insights from renowned real estate and personal development figures to enhance social proof.

Principles of Diversification

Diversification in real estate involves allocating investments across different property types, such as residential, commercial, and industrial properties, as well as various geographic regions. This approach helps mitigate risks associated with market fluctuations and ensures a steady income stream. Diversification also allows investors to capitalize on different market cycles, ensuring that downturns in one segment do not significantly impact the overall portfolio.

The Role of Economic Cycles in Diversification

Understanding economic cycles is crucial for real estate investors looking to build a resilient portfolio. Economic cycles are characterized by periods of growth, peak, contraction, and recovery, each presenting unique opportunities and risks for investors. By recognizing these phases, investors can strategically adjust their portfolios to maximize returns and minimize risks.

Example: Howard Marks on Economic Cycles

Howard Marks, co-founder of Oaktree Capital Management, emphasizes the importance of being attuned to market cycles. He suggests that investors who can anticipate shifts in the economy are better positioned to capitalize on opportunities during downturns and avoid overexposure during peaks. Marks advises investors to maintain flexibility and liquidity to adapt to changing economic conditions.

Balancing Property Types Across Cycles

David Lindahl advises diversifying investments across different property types to balance exposure during various economic cycles. For instance, during economic booms, commercial properties may experience higher demand, while residential properties tend to remain stable throughout all phases. Lindahl also suggests that emerging markets can offer significant growth opportunities during recovery phases, while stabilized markets provide security during contractions.

Example: Mixed-Use Developments for Cycle Stability

Mixed-use developments, which combine residential, commercial, and retail spaces, are gaining popularity for their resilience across different economic cycles. These properties offer multiple income streams, reducing the risk of relying on a single market segment. For example, a property with both office spaces and residential units can maintain cash flow even if one segment faces a downturn.

Incorporating Alternative Property Types

To further balance a portfolio, investors can explore alternative property types such as student housing, senior living, industrial spaces, and RV resorts. These sectors often operate independently of traditional market cycles and provide unique opportunities for diversification.

RV Resorts: A Growing Trend

One of the burgeoning trends in real estate investment is RV resorts. The popularity of RV travel has surged in recent years, driven by the desire for flexible, socially distanced travel options. RV resorts offer investors a unique opportunity to tap into a growing market segment that provides steady income through short-term stays and long-term leases.

Example: Sun Communities' Success in RV Resorts

Sun Communities, a publicly traded real estate investment trust (REIT), has successfully capitalized on the RV resort trend. The company owns and operates RV parks and resorts across the United States, generating significant revenue from both seasonal and year-round travelers. Their success highlights the potential profitability of investing in RV resorts.

Diversifying Beyond Traditional Property Types

In addition to RV resorts, investors can consider niche markets such as co-living spaces, medical office buildings, self-storage units, and build-to-rent communities. These property types offer different risk profiles and income streams, providing additional stability to a diversified portfolio.

Co-Living Spaces

Co-living spaces have gained popularity, particularly in urban areas where affordable housing options are limited. These properties offer shared living arrangements with private bedrooms and communal areas, catering to young professionals and digital nomads. The demand for co-living spaces has surged due to their affordability and community-focused living experience.

Example: The Collective in London

The Collective, a leading co-living operator, has developed multiple properties in cities like London and New York, providing residents with flexible leases and access to community events and amenities. This model has proven resilient, even during economic downturns, as it offers affordable and adaptable living solutions.

Build-to-Rent Communities

Build-to-rent (BTR) communities are purpose-built rental properties designed to provide long-term housing solutions. These communities often include amenities such as fitness centers, coworking spaces, and green areas, enhancing tenant satisfaction. BTR properties have gained traction in markets with housing shortages, offering a stable income stream for investors.

Example: Greystar's Expansion in BTR

Greystar, a global leader in rental housing, has significantly expanded its build-to-rent portfolio across the U.S. and Europe. The company focuses on creating high-quality rental communities that cater to a wide range of demographics, ensuring consistent demand and strong occupancy rates.

Medical Office Buildings

Medical office buildings (MOBs) are another alternative property type that offers stability. These properties are less affected by economic downturns, as healthcare services remain essential regardless of market conditions. MOBs typically attract long-term tenants, such as doctors and healthcare providers, ensuring a steady income stream.

Example: Healthcare Trust of America

Healthcare Trust of America, one of the largest publicly traded REITs focused on medical office buildings, has demonstrated the resilience of this property type. The trust's portfolio includes properties across major metropolitan areas, providing essential healthcare services to communities.

Self-Storage Units

Self-storage units are a popular investment option due to their low operating costs and consistent demand. These properties appeal to both residential and commercial tenants, providing flexible storage solutions. The rise of e-commerce has further driven demand for self-storage facilities.

Example: Public Storage

Public Storage, a leading self-storage operator, has consistently performed well through various economic cycles. The company's ability to maintain high occupancy rates and adjust rental prices based on demand makes self-storage a reliable addition to a diversified portfolio.

By incorporating these alternative property types, investors can enhance their portfolios' resilience and capitalize on emerging market trends. These investments align with the SMILE philosophy by addressing diverse community needs and promoting inclusivity in real estate offerings.

In addition to RV resorts, investors can consider niche markets such as co-living spaces, medical office buildings, and self-storage units. These property types offer different risk profiles and income streams, providing additional stability to a diversified portfolio.

Example: Sam Zell's Investment in Self-Storage

Sam Zell, a renowned real estate investor, has long advocated for investing in self-storage facilities due to their resilience during economic downturns. He highlights that self-storage units maintain steady demand regardless of market conditions, making them a reliable addition to a diversified portfolio.

Aligning Alternative Investments with the SMILE Philosophy

Incorporating alternative property types aligns with the SMILE philosophy by promoting inclusivity and experiential learning. Investing in diverse property types ensures that real estate offerings meet the evolving needs of various communities. For example, RV resorts cater to travelers seeking unique experiences, while senior living facilities provide essential services to aging populations. By diversifying into alternative properties, investors can achieve both financial success and positive community impact.

To further balance a portfolio, investors can explore alternative property types such as student housing, senior living, and industrial spaces. These sectors often operate independently of traditional market cycles. For instance, industrial properties, particularly warehouses, have seen steady demand due to the rise of e-commerce, regardless of broader economic fluctuations.

Example: Sam Zell on Industrial Properties

Sam Zell, a prominent real estate investor, has long championed the inclusion of industrial properties in a diversified portfolio. He highlights that industrial spaces, especially logistics hubs and warehouses, are less susceptible to economic downturns because of their essential role in supply chains. The rise of e-commerce has further cemented the demand for these properties, as companies require expansive warehouse spaces to meet online order fulfillment needs.

Case Study: Equity Industrial Partners

One of Zell's notable ventures, Equity Industrial Partners, focuses on acquiring and managing industrial assets across North America. The firm's strategy includes targeting logistics hubs in key transportation corridors, ensuring consistent demand from tenants in the retail and manufacturing sectors. This approach has led to steady cash flow and long-term property appreciation.

Adapting Industrial Properties for the Future

Zell also emphasizes the importance of adapting industrial properties to meet future demands. For example, the integration of automation and robotics in warehouses is becoming increasingly important. Properties that can accommodate advanced technologies, such as automated sorting systems and drone delivery zones, are more likely to attract high-quality tenants and command premium rents.

Alignment with the SMILE Philosophy

The SMILE philosophy—Safety, Morality, Inclusivity, Linguistic Clarity, and Experiential Learning—guides every aspect of investment strategy at SMILE Company LLC. The strategic direction taken by SMILE Company aligns closely with industry giants like Greystar, Blackstone, and Drysdale Properties, with a distinct focus on community impact. While these firms prioritize growth, stability, and community-centric projects, SMILE Company differentiates itself by putting an equal emphasis on emotional well-being—ensuring that every stakeholder can genuinely smile.

At SMILE Company, the belief is that "Smiles are as important as profits." This ethos means that tenants, employees, investors, and community members must all benefit from the company's projects. This people-first approach fosters trust, loyalty, and long-term relationships, ultimately contributing to financial success and community prosperity.

Comparative Example: Greystar's Focus on Community

Greystar, a leading global rental housing company, focuses heavily on community engagement and creating high-quality living environments. Their strategy aligns with the inclusivity aspect of the SMILE philosophy. However, where SMILE Company differentiates itself is in its unwavering commitment to ensuring emotional satisfaction and well-being—that every tenant, employee, and stakeholder leaves interactions with a positive experience.

Comparative Example: Blackstone's Ethical Investment Practices

Blackstone, one of the largest real estate investment firms, has recently shifted towards more sustainable and community-focused investments. Their initiatives in affordable housing and green building practices align with the safety and morality components of the SMILE philosophy. SMILE Company builds on this by embedding emotional well-being into its core mission, recognizing that financial returns and community happiness are interconnected.

Comparative Example: Drysdale Properties' Local Engagement

Drysdale Properties emphasizes local engagement and building strong relationships within the communities they serve. Their focus on localized investment aligns with the inclusivity and experiential learning aspects of the SMILE philosophy. SMILE Company enhances this approach by ensuring that these relationships are not only beneficial but also fulfilling—ensuring that every interaction contributes to a positive outcome for all involved.

By aligning with these established industry practices while adding a unique human-focused dimension, SMILE Company ensures that its projects are both profitable and impactful. The core belief that "every stakeholder must be able to smile" underscores the company's commitment to ethical, inclusive, and community-driven investment strategies. This holistic approach ensures that investments are not only financially successful but also contribute positively to societal well-being.

Investing in industrial properties aligns with the SMILE philosophy by promoting safety and inclusivity. Logistics hubs play a crucial role in supporting local economies by creating jobs and ensuring the smooth flow of goods. Additionally, the stability and resilience of industrial assets make them a safe and ethical investment choice for long-term portfolio growth.

Sam Zell, a prominent real estate investor, has long championed the inclusion of industrial properties in a diversified portfolio. He highlights that industrial spaces, especially logistics hubs and warehouses, are less susceptible to economic downturns because of their essential role in supply chains.

Adapting to Market Shifts

Investors should remain flexible and adapt their property types based on market trends. For example, after the COVID-19 pandemic, there was an increased demand for suburban properties and co-working spaces. Investors who diversified their portfolios to include these property types were better positioned to capitalize on changing consumer preferences.

Embracing Remote Work Trends

The rise of remote work has significantly influenced real estate investment strategies, prompting investors to adapt to new market dynamics. According to Jay Parsons, a prominent CRE analyst, the remote work trend is reshaping demand for both residential and commercial properties in profound ways.

Shift to Suburban and Rural Properties

With the flexibility to work from anywhere, many individuals are relocating from urban centers to suburban or rural areas in search of larger living spaces and a higher quality of life. This migration has increased demand for residential properties in these regions, making them attractive investment opportunities. Investors who anticipated this trend have seen significant returns by focusing on suburban developments.

Increased Demand for Flexible Workspaces

The hybrid work model has led to a surge in demand for flexible office solutions, such as co-working spaces. Jay Parsons highlights that the need for flexible workspaces has extended beyond major metropolitan areas to suburban and secondary markets, providing new opportunities for investors. Companies like WeWork have adjusted their strategies to capitalize on this trend by opening more locations in suburban areas.

Emphasis on Technologically Enhanced Properties

Remote workers require reliable internet connectivity and home office setups. Properties equipped with advanced technological infrastructure are in higher demand, prompting investors to prioritize tech enhancements in both residential and commercial real estate to attract tenants and buyers. Properties that offer smart home features and high-speed internet are becoming essential for retaining tenants in a competitive market.

Diversification into Secondary Markets

Parsons also notes the increasing attractiveness of secondary markets—smaller cities and towns experiencing growth due to remote work trends. These markets often offer lower entry costs and the potential for higher yields, aligning with the shift away from major metropolitan areas. Investors who have diversified into these markets are well-positioned to benefit from sustained demand.

The Rise of Emerging Secondary Markets

As population shifts continue, secondary markets are becoming hotbeds for real estate development and investment. Cities like Austin, Nashville, and Boise have seen unprecedented growth, driven by factors such as affordability, quality of life, and job market expansion. Investors who identified these trends early have reaped significant benefits.

Example: Austin's Tech Boom

Austin, Texas, has emerged as a prime example of a thriving secondary market. The city has become a hub for tech companies, attracting both talent and businesses. As a result, property values have surged, and rental demand has increased. Investors who entered the market early are now seeing substantial returns on their investments.

Affordable Housing in Secondary Markets

Secondary markets also present unique opportunities for affordable housing developments. With lower land and construction costs compared to primary markets, developers can build affordable units without compromising on quality. This aligns with the SMILE Philosophy's inclusivity component by providing more housing options for diverse demographics.

Aligning with the SMILE Philosophy

Diversification into secondary markets aligns with the SMILE Philosophy by promoting inclusivity and long-term stability. Investing in growing communities ensures that developments meet the needs of local populations and contribute to community well-being. Furthermore, by focusing on markets that are not oversaturated, investors can create sustainable, community-centric projects that foster positive social impact.

Parsons also notes the increasing attractiveness of secondary markets—smaller cities and towns experiencing growth due to remote work trends. These markets often offer lower entry costs and the potential for higher yields, aligning with the shift away from major metropolitan areas. Investors who have diversified into these markets are well-positioned to benefit from sustained demand.

Adaptation of Portfolio Management Strategies

The evolving real estate landscape necessitates that investors remain agile, regularly reassessing and adjusting their portfolios to align with current market conditions and emerging trends. This proactive approach ensures sustained profitability and resilience in a rapidly changing environment.

AI Integration and Its Impact on Portfolio Management

Over the next two years, the integration of Artificial Intelligence (AI) is expected to transform portfolio management strategies significantly. AI tools can analyze vast amounts of data in real-time, identifying trends and patterns that would be challenging for humans to detect. These insights will allow investors to make more informed decisions regarding property acquisition, rental pricing, and tenant retention.

For example, AI-driven platforms can predict market fluctuations and suggest optimal times for buying or selling properties. Property managers can also use AI to automate routine tasks such as maintenance scheduling, tenant communication, and rent collection, reducing operational costs and improving efficiency.

Example: AI-Powered Predictive Analytics

Platforms like RealPage and Yardi are already incorporating AI to provide predictive analytics. These tools help investors anticipate changes in property values, tenant behaviors, and local market conditions, allowing them to adjust their strategies proactively. As AI technology continues to evolve, these platforms will become even more accurate and reliable.

AI for Risk Management

AI can also enhance risk management by identifying potential risks before they become significant issues. For instance, AI can analyze lease agreements to detect discrepancies or flag properties that are more likely to experience tenant turnover. This proactive approach to risk management helps investors maintain portfolio stability and reduce losses.

AI-Driven Personalization

Another key benefit of AI integration is the ability to personalize tenant experiences. By analyzing tenant data, AI can recommend personalized leasing options, suggest property upgrades, and even predict which tenants are most likely to renew their leases. This level of personalization can improve tenant satisfaction and retention rates, ultimately boosting portfolio performance.

Aligning AI Integration with the SMILE Philosophy

The integration of AI aligns with the SMILE philosophy by promoting experiential learning and inclusivity. AI-driven insights enable investors to learn continuously from market data and adapt their strategies accordingly. Additionally, AI tools can enhance inclusivity by providing multilingual tenant portals and accessibility features that cater to diverse tenant needs.

By embracing AI technology, real estate investors can future-proof their portfolios and remain competitive in an increasingly data-driven industry. This forward-thinking approach ensures that portfolios are not only profitable but also aligned with ethical and inclusive practices.

The evolving real estate landscape necessitates that investors remain agile, regularly reassessing and adjusting their portfolios to align with current market conditions and emerging trends. This proactive approach ensures sustained profitability and resilience in a rapidly changing environment.

By acknowledging and responding to these trends, real estate investors can strategically position themselves to capitalize on the opportunities presented by the remote work revolution.

One of the significant shifts in recent years is the rise of remote work, which has reshaped demand for both residential and commercial properties. Investors who adapted to this trend by investing in properties with home office spaces, high-speed internet infrastructure, and flexible layouts saw increased demand from tenants. Additionally, co-working spaces in suburban areas have gained popularity as remote workers seek professional environments closer to home.

Example: WeWork's Shift to Suburban Markets

WeWork, a global leader in flexible workspaces, has pivoted its strategy to include more suburban locations to cater to remote workers. This shift reflects the growing demand for co-working spaces outside major metropolitan areas, providing investors with new opportunities to diversify their portfolios.

Green and Sustainable Properties

Another market shift is the growing demand for green and sustainable properties. Investors who adapted by incorporating eco-friendly features such as solar panels, energy-efficient appliances, and green roofs have seen increased tenant interest and higher property values. Sustainability is no longer a luxury but a necessity, and properties that meet these standards are more likely to attract long-term tenants.

Beyond Traditional Green Features

Modern green properties go beyond basic energy efficiency. Features such as rainwater harvesting systems, solar energy storage solutions, and smart irrigation systems are becoming commonplace in new developments. Additionally, properties that incorporate biophilic designs—which integrate natural elements like green walls and rooftop gardens—have been shown to improve tenant well-being and productivity.

Example: The Edge in Amsterdam

One notable example of a highly sustainable property is The Edge in Amsterdam, considered one of the most sustainable office buildings in the world. The building incorporates smart lighting systems, solar energy, and a rainwater harvesting system to minimize its environmental footprint. The success of The Edge demonstrates that sustainability can be both financially viable and appealing to tenants.

Regulatory Pressure and Incentives

Governments worldwide are implementing stricter regulations and offering incentives to encourage sustainable building practices. For example, the U.S. government offers tax credits and grants for green building initiatives, making it financially advantageous for investors to adopt sustainable practices. Similarly, the European Union has set ambitious carbon reduction targets, prompting developers to prioritize sustainability in their projects.

Impact of the Upcoming Trump Presidency on Real Estate Regulations

The anticipated return of Donald Trump to the presidency is expected to bring significant changes to real estate regulations in the United States. Known for his pro-business stance, Trump has often advocated for reducing bureaucracy and cutting down on excessive building fees and regulations that he believes stifle development and economic growth. His administration is likely to focus on deregulation, making it easier for developers to obtain permits and complete projects more efficiently.

One of the key areas where Trump's policies could have a profound impact is the cost to build affordable housing. By cutting red tape and reducing regulatory burdens, developers may find it more cost-effective to pursue affordable housing projects. This could include reducing zoning restrictions, streamlining the approval process for new developments, and offering tax incentives for affordable housing construction.

Aligning Affordable Housing with the SMILE Philosophy

Affordable housing aligns closely with the inclusivity component of the SMILE Philosophy. By making it easier for developers to build affordable units, more individuals and families can access quality housing options. Trump's focus on reducing bureaucratic hurdles and lowering costs for developers complements SMILE's goal of creating community-centric projects that prioritize both financial returns and social impact.

Additionally, by promoting deregulation and offering incentives for affordable housing, a Trump administration could help bridge the gap between market-rate and affordable units, fostering more diverse and inclusive communities. This approach ensures that all stakeholders—tenants, developers, and investors—benefit from housing developments that align with both economic and ethical principles.

Case Study: Opportunity Zones and Affordable Housing

During Trump's first term, the Opportunity Zones program encouraged investment in economically distressed areas. Developers who invested in these areas received tax incentives, making it more feasible to build affordable housing. A future Trump administration could expand on this program to further incentivize affordable housing development, aligning with the SMILE Philosophy's focus on community well-being and economic prosperity.

By anticipating these regulatory changes and aligning their strategies with both the SMILE Philosophy and potential policy shifts, investors can position themselves for long-term success in an evolving market.

Aligning the SMILE Philosophy with Trump's Views on Real Estate

The SMILE Philosophy—Safety, Morality, Inclusivity, Linguistic Clarity, and Experiential Learning—aligns with some of Trump's known opinions on real estate. Trump has long advocated for reducing bureaucratic hurdles that can slow down development projects. This focus on efficiency aligns with the SMILE principle of experiential learning, where continuous improvement and adaptation are key to success.

Moreover, Trump's stance on making real estate more accessible through reduced fees and taxes resonates with the inclusivity component of the SMILE Philosophy. By lowering entry barriers, more investors and developers can participate in real estate projects, leading to diverse and community-centric developments.

"Smiles Are as Important as Profits"

While Trump's approach to real estate often emphasizes profitability, SMILE Company LLC differentiates itself by equally prioritizing emotional well-being. The belief that "smiles are as important as profits" ensures that every stakeholder—from tenants to investors—benefits from a project. This people-first approach fosters stronger community ties and long-term loyalty, something that can complement Trump's deregulatory stance by ensuring that developments remain ethical and beneficial to all parties involved.

Case Study: Deregulation and Economic Growth

During Trump's first term, deregulation initiatives contributed to economic growth by reducing the costs associated with real estate development. For example, changes to the Opportunity Zones program encouraged investment in economically distressed areas, leading to job creation and improved infrastructure. Similar policies could be expected in a future Trump administration, aligning with SMILE's goal of promoting community prosperity through responsible investment.

By anticipating these regulatory changes and aligning their strategies with both the SMILE Philosophy and potential policy shifts, investors can position themselves for long-term success in an evolving market.

Governments worldwide are implementing stricter regulations and offering incentives to encourage sustainable building practices. For example, the U.S. government offers tax credits and grants for green building initiatives, making it financially advantageous for investors to adopt sustainable practices. Similarly, the European Union has set ambitious carbon reduction targets, prompting developers to prioritize sustainability in their projects.

Sustainability as a Competitive Advantage

Investors who incorporate sustainable features into their properties can achieve a competitive advantage. Properties with green certifications, such as LEED (Leadership in Energy and Environmental Design), often command higher rents and attract environmentally conscious tenants. As more tenants prioritize eco-friendly living and working environments, sustainability will become a key factor in property selection.

Aligning Sustainability with the SMILE Philosophy

Sustainable properties align with the SMILE philosophy by promoting safety, morality, and experiential learning. Eco-friendly buildings create healthier living and working environments, contributing to tenant well-being and safety. By adopting sustainable practices, investors demonstrate a commitment to ethical investing, ensuring that their properties have a positive impact on both communities and the planet.

Another market shift is the growing demand for green and sustainable properties. Investors who adapted by incorporating eco-friendly features such as solar panels, energy-efficient appliances, and green roofs have seen increased tenant interest and higher property values. Sustainability is no longer a luxury but a necessity, and properties that meet these standards are more likely to attract long-term tenants.

Example: Blackstone's Investment in Sustainable Assets

Blackstone, one of the largest real estate investment firms, has made significant investments in sustainable properties. The firm's commitment to ESG (Environmental, Social, and Governance) principles has positioned it as a leader in green real estate. By adapting to this market shift, Blackstone has enhanced its portfolio's resilience and long-term profitability.

Adapting to Market Shifts

Adapting to market shifts aligns with the SMILE philosophy by promoting experiential learning and inclusivity. Investors who stay informed about changing trends can make data-driven decisions that benefit their portfolios and the communities they serve. By embracing innovation and inclusivity, investors can create resilient, future-proof portfolios that align with both financial goals and social responsibility.

Investors should remain flexible and adapt their property types based on market trends. For example, after the COVID-19 pandemic, there was an increased demand for suburban properties and co-working spaces. Investors who diversified their portfolios to include these property types were better positioned to capitalize on changing consumer preferences.

Balancing Property Types

Balancing property types aligns with the SMILE philosophy by promoting safety and inclusivity. Including a variety of property types ensures that investors provide housing and commercial solutions that meet diverse community needs. Additionally, balancing risk and reward promotes long-term stability, benefiting both investors and the communities they serve.

David Lindahl advises diversifying investments across different property types to balance exposure during various economic cycles. For instance, during economic booms, commercial properties may experience higher demand, while residential properties tend to remain stable throughout all phases. Lindahl also suggests that emerging markets can offer significant growth opportunities during recovery phases, while stabilized markets provide security during contractions.

Case Study: Resilient Portfolios During Economic Downturns

During the 2008 financial crisis, investors with diversified portfolios that included a mix of stabilized residential properties and high-growth commercial assets in emerging markets were better able to weather the downturn. For example, real estate firms that held assets across various geographic locations and property types saw fewer overall losses compared to those with concentrated portfolios.

Lessons from the COVID-19 Pandemic

The COVID-19 pandemic presented another significant economic challenge that tested the resilience of real estate portfolios. Investors who had diversified their portfolios across various property types, including suburban residential units, industrial properties, and short-term rentals, fared better than those focused solely on urban office spaces. For instance, industrial properties, particularly warehouses, saw increased demand as e-commerce boomed during the pandemic, providing a steady income stream for investors.

Example: Resilient Performance of Industrial REITs

Industrial real estate investment trusts (REITs), such as Prologis, demonstrated resilience during economic downturns. By focusing on logistics and warehouse spaces, these REITs capitalized on the growing demand for e-commerce and supply chain solutions. Prologis reported stable occupancy rates and rent collections even during the height of the pandemic, showcasing the importance of portfolio diversification.

Navigating Market Shifts with Flexible Strategies

Investors who adopt flexible strategies and remain agile during economic downturns can better manage risks and capitalize on new opportunities. For example, shifting investments to secondary markets or transitioning office spaces into co-working hubs can help offset losses in other areas of the portfolio. Flexibility and adaptability are key traits of resilient investors.

Example: Blackstone's Adaptive Portfolio Management

Blackstone, one of the world's largest real estate investment firms, exemplifies adaptive portfolio management. During periods of economic uncertainty, Blackstone has strategically shifted its focus toward sectors that demonstrate resilience, such as logistics, life sciences, and data centers. This adaptability has allowed the firm to maintain strong performance even during economic downturns.

Aligning Resilience with the SMILE Philosophy

Resilient portfolios align with the SMILE Philosophy by promoting safety and experiential learning. By diversifying across property types and geographic regions, investors ensure the long-term safety of their investments. Additionally, the experiential learning component encourages investors to continuously adapt and improve their strategies based on market conditions, ensuring sustainable success even in challenging economic times.

During the 2008 financial crisis, investors with diversified portfolios that included a mix of stabilized residential properties and high-growth commercial assets in emerging markets were better able to weather the downturn. For example, real estate firms that held assets across various geographic locations and property types saw fewer overall losses compared to those with concentrated portfolios.

Applying the SMILE Philosophy to Economic Cycles

The SMILE philosophy aligns well with economic cycle diversification. By prioritizing safety and morality, investors can make ethical choices during both peaks and downturns, ensuring long-term stability. Inclusivity in portfolio management also means considering diverse markets and demographics, which can offer unique growth opportunities during different phases of the cycle.

Long-Term Perspective in Economic Cycles

Investors who adopt a long-term perspective and remain patient through economic cycles often see greater success. Dan Sullivan, a renowned personal development coach, advises focusing on long-term goals and adapting to changes rather than reacting emotionally to short-term market fluctuations. This mindset can help investors maintain resilience and continue to grow their portfolios regardless of economic conditions.

David Lindahl, a prominent real estate investor, emphasizes the importance of understanding economic cycles when diversifying a portfolio. By investing in both stabilized markets and emerging markets, investors can balance risk and growth potential. Lindahl advocates for a diversified approach that includes properties in various stages of the market cycle to reduce vulnerability to economic downturns.

Balancing Risk and Reward

Diversification also involves balancing risk and reward by including both high-risk, high-reward properties and more stable, income-generating assets. For instance, investing in a mix of Class A, B, and C properties can help achieve this balance. While Class A properties offer lower risk and steady returns, Class B and C properties may provide higher yields but come with increased management demands.

Emerging Trends in Balancing Risk and Reward

The real estate landscape is evolving, with new asset classes emerging that offer unique risk-reward profiles. For example, build-to-rent communities and co-living spaces provide higher potential yields but may require more active management compared to traditional rental properties. Similarly, investing in industrial properties such as warehouses and data centers has become increasingly attractive due to the rise of e-commerce and digital infrastructure needs.

Example: Investing in Data Centers

Data centers have become a popular investment due to the growing demand for cloud services and digital infrastructure. These properties offer a relatively stable income stream, as companies are willing to pay premium rents for secure, reliable data storage solutions. While the initial investment can be significant, the long-term rewards often outweigh the risks.

Risk Mitigation Through Diversification

Balancing risk and reward also involves mitigating risks through geographic and sector diversification. For instance, investors who spread their portfolios across different regions and property types are better positioned to weather economic downturns. Investing in recession-resistant sectors, such as healthcare and self-storage, can further enhance portfolio resilience.

Example: Healthcare Real Estate

Healthcare real estate, including medical office buildings and senior living facilities, has proven to be resilient during economic downturns. These properties provide essential services that remain in demand regardless of market conditions. Investing in this sector can offer a steady income stream with relatively low risk.

Aligning with the SMILE Philosophy

Balancing risk and reward aligns with the SMILE Philosophy by promoting safety and experiential learning. By diversifying portfolios and managing risks proactively, investors can create sustainable, long-term success. Additionally, focusing on inclusive investments ensures that diverse communities benefit from real estate developments, contributing to positive societal impact.

Diversification also involves balancing risk and reward by including both high-risk, high-reward properties and more stable, income-generating assets. For instance, investing in a mix of Class A, B, and C properties can help achieve this balance. While Class A properties offer lower risk and steady returns, Class B and C properties may provide higher yields but come with increased management demands.

Example: Ray Dalio's Diversification Principles

Ray Dalio, founder of Bridgewater Associates, often stresses the importance of diversification in investment portfolios. He believes that spreading investments across uncorrelated assets reduces risk and enhances long-term returns. Applying Dalio's principles to real estate, investors can achieve a more resilient portfolio by investing in properties across different asset classes, locations, and markets.

Importance of Geographic Diversification

Geographic diversification is another key component of a well-rounded portfolio. Investing in different regions protects investors from localized economic shocks. For example, an investor with properties in both urban and suburban areas can benefit from the migration trends that affect demand in each type of location.

Emerging Opportunities in Secondary and Tertiary Markets

Expanding into secondary and tertiary markets has become increasingly attractive as these areas often offer lower entry costs, higher growth potential, and less competition compared to primary markets. Cities like Boise, Raleigh, and Chattanooga are examples of emerging markets that have seen significant population and economic growth, creating lucrative opportunities for real estate investors.

Case Study: The Growth of Boise, Idaho

Boise has transformed from a quiet town into a thriving metropolitan area. The city's strong job market, high quality of life, and affordability have attracted both residents and businesses. Investors who entered the Boise market early have seen substantial property appreciation and rental demand, demonstrating the benefits of geographic expansion.

International Geographic Diversification

For investors seeking further diversification, exploring international markets can provide additional protection against localized economic downturns. Markets in Southeast Asia, Eastern Europe, and Latin America are experiencing rapid growth and urbanization, offering attractive opportunities for real estate investment.

Example: Investing in Lisbon, Portugal

Lisbon has become a hotspot for international real estate investment due to its favorable tax policies, high rental yields, and growing tourism sector. Investors who expanded into this market have capitalized on the city's popularity among digital nomads and retirees, ensuring steady returns and portfolio growth.

George Knowlton

Aligning Geographic Expansion with the SMILE Philosophy

The SMILE Philosophy emphasizes inclusivity and long-term value creation, which aligns with geographic diversification strategies. By investing in various regions, real estate professionals can create diverse and resilient portfolios that cater to a wide range of community needs. Expanding into underserved or emerging areas also promotes economic development, contributing to the overall well-being of the communities involved.

By applying these principles, investors can create a portfolio that is resilient to market changes and capable of delivering long-term financial success.

Geographic diversification is another key component of a well-rounded portfolio. Investing in different regions protects investors from localized economic shocks. For example, an investor with properties in both urban and suburban areas can benefit from the migration trends that affect demand in each type of location.

Example: Barbara Corcoran on Geographic Expansion

Barbara Corcoran, a real estate mogul, advises investors to explore opportunities in different geographic regions to maximize growth. She highlights that cities experiencing population growth or economic revitalization present lucrative investment opportunities. By expanding their geographic footprint, investors can tap into emerging markets and diversify their income sources.

By applying these principles, investors can create a portfolio that is resilient to market changes and capable of delivering long-term financial success.

Diversification in real estate involves allocating investments across different property types, such as residential, commercial, and industrial properties, as well as various geographic regions. This approach helps mitigate risks associated with market fluctuations and ensures a steady income stream.

Example: Ken McElroy's Approach to Diversification

Ken McElroy, a leading real estate investor and author, advocates for diversification as a key strategy for building wealth. He emphasizes the importance of balancing a portfolio with a mix of multifamily units, commercial spaces, and storage facilities. By diversifying, McElroy has managed to maintain consistent cash flow even during economic downturns.

Example: Barbara Corcoran on Diversifying Income Streams

Barbara Corcoran, founder of The Corcoran Group, highlights the value of diversifying income streams in real estate. She advises investors to look beyond traditional rental properties and explore alternative investments such as short-term rentals, co-working spaces, and mixed-use developments. Corcoran's diversified approach has helped her navigate market challenges and achieve long-term success.

Portfolio Management Techniques

Effective portfolio management requires regular performance reviews, market analysis, and strategic adjustments to maximize returns. Leveraging technology and data analytics can provide valuable insights into portfolio performance and help investors make informed decisions.

AI-Driven Portfolio Management

The integration of artificial intelligence (AI) is transforming portfolio management techniques. AI tools can analyze vast amounts of data in real-time, helping investors predict market trends, optimize rental pricing, and identify underperforming assets. These tools enable investors to automate routine tasks, such as rent collection and maintenance scheduling, reducing operational costs and improving efficiency.

Example: AI-Enhanced Property Insights

Platforms like Yardi and RealPage are incorporating AI to offer predictive insights into property performance and tenant behavior. By using AI algorithms, these platforms can recommend strategic adjustments to improve portfolio profitability and reduce risks associated with vacancies and maintenance issues.

Scenario Planning and Risk Management

Scenario planning is another critical aspect of portfolio management. By using data-driven models, investors can simulate different economic scenarios and assess their impact on property values and cash flows. This approach allows investors to prepare for potential downturns and adjust their strategies accordingly.

Example: Blackstone's Use of Scenario Planning

Blackstone, one of the largest real estate investment firms, uses scenario planning to manage its diverse portfolio. By anticipating various market conditions, the firm can proactively adjust its investments to maintain stable returns and minimize risks.

Technology-Enabled Portfolio Reviews

Regular portfolio reviews are essential for identifying underperforming assets and reallocating resources to higher-yield investments. Technology tools, such as dashboards and automated reporting systems, streamline the review process by providing real-time data and performance metrics. This enables investors to make data-driven decisions quickly and efficiently.

AI-Driven Dashboards for Comprehensive Insights

The use of AI-driven dashboards allows investors to gain comprehensive insights into their portfolios in real time. These platforms can track key performance indicators (KPIs) such as occupancy rates, rental income, and maintenance costs. By automating the data collection process, investors can save time and focus on strategic decision-making. Companies like RealPage and Yardi have integrated AI capabilities into their dashboards to provide predictive analytics and actionable recommendations.

Example: Predictive Maintenance Alerts

One innovative feature of technology-enabled portfolio reviews is predictive maintenance alerts. These alerts use IoT sensors to monitor building systems and detect potential issues before they become costly repairs. For example, a property management system can notify investors when an HVAC system requires maintenance based on usage data, reducing downtime and repair costs.

Blockchain for Transparent Reporting

Blockchain technology is another emerging tool in portfolio reviews. By using blockchain for property management, investors can ensure that all transactions and reports are transparent and tamper-proof. This can be particularly valuable for multi-property portfolios where maintaining accurate records across various assets is challenging. Blockchain's immutable ledger provides an added layer of security and trust for portfolio reviews.

Aligning with the SMILE Philosophy

Technology-enabled portfolio reviews align with the SMILE Philosophy by promoting safety, experiential learning, and inclusivity. Automated reporting tools enhance the safety of investments by reducing the risk of human error in data collection. Additionally, continuous learning through real-time analytics allows investors to adapt their strategies based on market trends. By incorporating inclusive tools, such as multilingual dashboards, investors can ensure that all stakeholders, regardless of language or technical expertise, can understand and participate in portfolio management.

Regular portfolio reviews are essential for identifying underperforming assets and reallocating resources to higher-yield investments. Technology tools, such as dashboards and automated reporting systems, streamline the review process by providing real-time data and performance metrics. This enables investors to make data-driven decisions quickly and efficiently.

Aligning Portfolio Management with the SMILE Philosophy

The SMILE Philosophy promotes experiential learning and inclusivity, both of which are integral to effective portfolio management. By continuously analyzing data and adapting strategies, investors can learn from their experiences and improve their decision-making processes. Additionally, by prioritizing community-focused investments, investors ensure that their portfolios contribute to societal well-being and align with ethical practices.

Emerging Trends in Portfolio Management

Emerging trends such as blockchain technology and tokenization are expected to further revolutionize portfolio management. These innovations can enhance transparency, liquidity, and accessibility, allowing more investors to participate in real estate markets and diversify their holdings. For example, tokenization enables fractional ownership of properties, making real estate investments more accessible to a broader audience and aligning with the inclusivity principle of the SMILE Philosophy.

Effective portfolio management requires regular performance reviews, market analysis, and strategic adjustments to maximize returns. Leveraging technology and data analytics can provide valuable insights into portfolio performance and help investors make informed decisions.

Example: Using Data Analytics for Portfolio Optimization

Platforms like RealPage and AppFolio offer data-driven tools that help investors monitor property performance, occupancy rates, and market trends. These insights enable investors to adjust their strategies proactively and optimize their portfolios for maximum profitability.

Example: David Lindahl's Strategy for Market Cycles

David Lindahl, a renowned real estate investor and author of "Emerging Markets," stresses the importance of understanding market cycles when managing a diversified portfolio. His strategy involves identifying and investing in emerging markets before they reach their peak, allowing investors to maximize growth potential and minimize risks associated with market saturation.

Lindahl's approach emphasizes the timing of investments in various market phases—recovery, expansion, hyper-supply, and recession. He advises investors to enter markets during the recovery phase, when property values are still low and demand is beginning to increase, and exit or reposition investments as markets approach hyper-supply to avoid the risk of declining values.

Applying the Strategy to Different Property Types

Lindahl also highlights the importance of diversifying property types across different market cycles. For example, during an expansion phase, multifamily units and commercial properties tend to perform well due to increased demand and economic growth. However, in a recession phase, investors might focus on more stable assets like self-storage facilities or affordable housing, which tend to maintain steady demand even in challenging economic conditions.

Case Study: Lindahl's Investment in Emerging Markets

A notable example of Lindahl's strategy is his investment in the Dallas-Fort Worth area during its recovery phase. By identifying early signs of population growth and job market expansion, Lindahl acquired multifamily properties at relatively low prices. Over time, these properties appreciated significantly in value as the market entered its expansion phase, resulting in substantial returns.

Aligning Lindahl's Strategy with the SMILE Philosophy

Lindahl's strategy aligns well with the SMILE Philosophy, particularly in terms of experiential learning and safety. By studying market cycles and learning from past economic trends, investors can make informed decisions that protect their portfolios from market volatility. Additionally, investing in emerging markets supports community growth and economic development, aligning with SMILE's commitment to inclusivity and long-term value creation.

David Lindahl, a renowned real estate investor and author of "Emerging Markets," stresses the importance of understanding market cycles when managing a diversified portfolio.

Conclusion

As we have explored throughout this chapter, building and managing a diversified real estate portfolio is a crucial strategy for long-term success in an ever-evolving market. The importance of balancing risk and reward, adapting to market shifts, and embracing geographic diversification cannot be overstated. With the rise of technology-enabled portfolio management and emerging asset classes, investors have more tools than ever to enhance their strategies and achieve sustainable growth.

The SMILE Philosophy remains at the core of these approaches, emphasizing safety, morality, inclusivity, linguistic clarity, and experiential learning. By aligning their investment strategies with these values, investors can not only maximize financial returns but also contribute positively to the communities they serve.

As we move forward to Chapter 8, we will delve deeper into the practical applications of these strategies. We will explore how to implement actionable steps for community-centric investments and discuss the role of leadership and vision in shaping future developments. Get ready to take your investment journey to the next level as we continue to build towards a future of inclusive, sustainable, and resilient real estate.

Chapter 8
Financing Strategies and Opportunities

In the fast-paced world of real estate investing, financing is not just a tool to acquire property; it's a gateway to building wealth and creating lasting community impact. It encompasses a variety of strategies, each offering unique pathways to achieve financial freedom and social responsibility. For example, renowned investor Ken McElroy, author of *The ABCs of Real Estate Investing*, advocates for a practical approach to financing that focuses on positive cash flow and long-term sustainability. McElroy's philosophy aligns with the SMILE values by emphasizing the importance of ethical investing practices that benefit both investors and the communities they serve.

Real World Example: McElroy's investment firm, MC Companies, has been involved in numerous projects that provide affordable housing options while incorporating sustainable practices, such as energy-efficient designs and community-building programs. This approach demonstrates that financing strategies can be both profitable and socially responsible, reflecting the values of inclusivity and experiential learning embedded in the SMILE philosophy.

Financing is the lifeblood of real estate investing. Whether you're a seasoned investor or just starting out, understanding various financing strategies is crucial for success. It's not just about securing funds; it's about empowering yourself with the right financial tools to unlock opportunities. As Sophia Hart would remind us, financing should be approached with a growth mindset—focusing on building both wealth and community impact. In this chapter, we will explore traditional and innovative financing methods, with insights from some of the most respected figures in real estate and personal development. We'll also examine how these strategies align with the core SMILE values, ensuring that every investment decision contributes positively to your portfolio and the communities you serve.

Exploring Financing Options

Securing financing is one of the most significant hurdles in real estate investing, but it doesn't have to be an intimidating process. Think of financing as building a bridge to your future goals—each plank you lay brings you closer to your destination. By approaching financing with a clear strategy and a willingness to adapt, you can create sustainable pathways to success. As Sophia Hart often advocates, understanding your financing options empowers you to make informed decisions that balance financial growth with community impact.

Renowned real estate investor Warren Buffett emphasizes the importance of long-term value creation when financing real estate ventures. He believes in securing investments that offer sustainable returns over time. Buffett's philosophy resonates with the SMILE values by advocating for ethical investment decisions that positively impact communities. For instance, his investment in real estate-focused REITs demonstrates his commitment to diversified, long-term strategies that support economic growth and community stability.

Real World Example: In 2022, a partnership between Berkshire Hathaway and a sustainable housing initiative led to the development of affordable, energy-efficient homes in underserved areas. This project aligns with the SMILE philosophy by promoting inclusivity and sustainability while delivering solid returns to investors.

Securing financing is one of the most significant hurdles in real estate investing, but it doesn't have to be an intimidating process. Think of financing as building a bridge to your future goals—each plank you lay brings you closer to your destination. By approaching financing with a clear strategy and a willingness to adapt, you can create sustainable pathways to success. As Sophia Hart often advocates, understanding your financing options empowers you to make informed decisions that balance financial growth with community impact.

One of the first steps in real estate investment is securing the right financing. Traditional bank loans, private lenders, and modern crowdfunding platforms each offer unique advantages and limitations. Robert Kiyosaki, author of *Rich Dad Poor Dad*, emphasizes the importance of leveraging other people's money (OPM) to build wealth in real estate, specifically noting in Chapter 5 that mastering OPM can significantly increase one's investment potential without excessive personal risk. He advises investors to focus on financing strategies that maximize returns without overextending their risk.

Traditional Financing Methods

Traditional financing methods, such as bank loans and private lenders, have long been the backbone of real estate investments. These methods offer stability, predictability, and well-established processes that investors can rely on. However, success with traditional financing requires more than just securing a loan; it demands a strategic approach to building long-term relationships with lenders and understanding the nuances of different loan products.

Barbara Corcoran, a prominent real estate mogul and investor on *Shark Tank*, highlights the importance of maintaining a strong credit profile and a comprehensive business plan when approaching traditional lenders. Corcoran stresses that the key to securing favorable terms lies in demonstrating reliability and a clear vision for your projects.

Real World Example: In 2021, a family-owned real estate firm in Texas used a combination of bank loans and private lenders to finance a mixed-use development project. By leveraging their long-standing relationship with a local bank, they secured lower interest rates and favorable repayment terms, which allowed them to allocate more funds toward sustainable building practices and community amenities. This approach not only ensured the project's profitability but also strengthened the firm's reputation in the local community.

Key Takeaways from Traditional Financing:

- Maintain a solid credit profile to build trust with lenders.
- Build long-term relationships with financial institutions to access better loan products.
- Leverage assets strategically to negotiate favorable terms and lower interest rates.

Bank loans remain a popular choice for investors due to their stability and predictability. However, securing a loan requires a strong credit score, a comprehensive business plan, and a clear repayment strategy. Barbara Corcoran, a prominent real estate mogul and investor on *Shark Tank*, highlights the importance of building relationships with lenders to secure favorable terms.

Modern Crowdfunding Methods

Crowdfunding has revolutionized the way real estate projects are funded. Platforms like Fundrise and RealtyMogul allow investors to pool resources for larger projects, reducing individual financial burdens. The global real estate crowdfunding market is expected to reach around $230 billion by 2030, reflecting its growing significance in the investment landscape.

One of the most appealing aspects of crowdfunding is its ability to democratize real estate investing by lowering the barriers to entry. Investors who may not have access to large amounts of capital can participate in substantial projects by contributing smaller amounts. This inclusivity aligns with the SMILE philosophy, particularly the values of Morality and Inclusivity.

Popular Story: Doorvest, a homeownership investment platform, successfully raised over $5 million from 574 investors through a crowdfunding campaign on Wefunder in 2023. This achievement demonstrates the increasing interest in real estate crowdfunding and its potential to democratize property investment.

Additionally, platforms such as Crowdstreet have enabled institutional-quality real estate projects to be funded by a diverse group of investors. In 2022, Crowdstreet facilitated a $30 million project for a mixed-use development in Oregon. This project incorporated sustainable building practices and community-focused amenities, reflecting the Experiential learning aspect of the SMILE philosophy by creating properties that serve the broader community's needs.

Grant Cardone, a well-known real estate investor and author of *The 10X Rule*, has promoted the concept of leveraging capital through partnerships and private equity for multifamily housing expansion, though direct references to his use of crowdfunding are not well-documented. It is advisable to cross-reference his specific financing strategies with verified sources. Cardone emphasizes that crowdfunding democratizes real estate investing, making it accessible to those with limited capital.

Popular Story: A developer in San Francisco raised $3 million through a combination of private equity and crowdfunding for a multifamily housing project, demonstrating the power of modern financing methods.

Innovative Funding Methods

Beyond traditional loans and crowdfunding, investors can explore innovative funding strategies such as joint ventures, partnerships, and real estate investment groups (REIGs). These methods reduce individual financial burdens and allow investors to tackle larger projects while sharing the risks and rewards.

Tony Robbins, a renowned life coach and business strategist, often speaks about the power of strategic partnerships, particularly in his book *Unshakeable*, where he highlights the importance of aligning with like-minded individuals to achieve greater success in ventures, including real estate. In his seminars, Robbins stresses that partnerships can amplify success by combining resources, expertise, and networks.

Renowned investor Sam Zell, often referred to as the "Grave Dancer" for his ability to identify and capitalize on undervalued properties, is a prime example of innovative funding in action. Zell has long advocated for opportunistic joint ventures that leverage creative financing structures to minimize risk while maximizing returns. His approach often involves forming strategic partnerships with institutional investors to fund large-scale developments or acquisitions.

Real World Example: In 2020, Zell's firm, Equity Residential, partnered with a pension fund to acquire a mixed-use development in a prime urban location. By sharing the financial responsibilities and risks, both parties benefited from the deal's success, achieving stable returns and contributing to the revitalization of the local community.

Benefits of Joint Ventures and Partnerships:

- Shared financial responsibilities reduce individual risk.
- Access to larger projects that might be unattainable individually.
- Diversification of risk through collaboration.
- Opportunity to leverage partners' expertise and networks.

These innovative funding methods align with the SMILE philosophy by promoting Inclusivity through shared investment opportunities and Experiential learning through collaborative projects. Investors who embrace these methods can build not only financial wealth but also lasting partnerships and community impact.

Beyond traditional loans and crowdfunding, investors can explore innovative funding strategies such as joint ventures, partnerships, and real estate investment groups (REIGs). These methods reduce individual financial burdens and allow investors to tackle larger projects.

Pain Point Solution: Overcoming High Upfront Costs

One common concern among new investors is the high upfront cost of real estate investments. However, alternative financing solutions such as real estate investment trusts (REITs), fractional ownership platforms, lease-option agreements, and hard money loans offer entry points with lower individual capital requirements.

Brandon Turner, co-host of the *BiggerPockets Podcast*, advises new investors to start small and gradually scale their portfolio, as discussed in Episode 371, where he shares insights on building wealth through incremental property acquisitions and practical strategies for beginners. Turner emphasizes the power of creative financing, such as seller financing, using private lenders, or forming joint ventures to minimize the need for large cash reserves. He also highlights the importance of leveraging partnerships and networks to access unique opportunities that may not be available through traditional financing methods.

Real World Example: In 2022, a first-time investor in Denver utilized a lease-option agreement to acquire a duplex with minimal upfront capital. By negotiating terms that allowed a portion of the rent to be applied toward the purchase price, the investor secured the property without a traditional mortgage. This creative approach demonstrates that financial limitations can be overcome with strategic thinking.

In another example, a group of investors in California formed a real estate investment group to pool their resources and acquire a commercial property. By collectively securing a hard money loan, they were able to close the deal quickly and renovate the property to increase its value, generating significant returns for all members of the group.

Analogy: Financing a project is like pooling resources for a group vacation. Everyone contributes, and together you can achieve more than you could alone, proving that lack of individual capital is no excuse for missing out on lucrative investment opportunities.

Case Study: Leveraging Financing to Scale

Sarah, a real estate investor from Chicago, started her journey with a small duplex financed through a traditional bank loan. By reinvesting her profits and utilizing innovative financing methods, including joint ventures and private equity, Sarah scaled her portfolio to over 50 properties within a decade. Her success story was featured in *Forbes* as a testament to the power of creative financing and the importance of building strong partnerships. Sarah credits her success to consistently identifying value-add opportunities and using creative financing structures to maximize returns while benefiting local communities.

Case Study: James and Rebecca, a couple from Austin, Texas, faced difficulties securing traditional financing for their first commercial property. Instead of giving up, they explored alternative financing options, including seller financing and a joint venture with a local investment group. This creative approach allowed them to acquire a mixed-use property in a growing neighborhood. By offering affordable retail spaces to local businesses and implementing sustainable building practices, they not only achieved financial success but also contributed to the area's economic growth. Their story showcases how innovative financing can lead to both profitability and positive community impact.

Maximizing Returns Through Smart Financing

Successful investors understand that financing isn't just about securing funds; it's about optimizing those funds for maximum returns. Dave Ramsey, a personal finance expert, cautions against over-leveraging and advocates for smart debt management, particularly in his book *The Total Money Makeover*, where he emphasizes the importance of living debt-free and carefully managing any necessary debt to avoid financial pitfalls. He suggests maintaining a healthy balance between equity and debt to ensure long-term financial stability.

In addition to Ramsey's approach, billionaire real estate investor Sam Zell stresses the importance of opportunistic refinancing. Zell believes that timing is key when refinancing properties, advocating for taking advantage of favorable interest rates and using the resulting liquidity to reinvest in value-add projects. This approach aligns with the SMILE philosophy by ensuring investments are sustainable and contribute positively to communities.

Actionable Tips for Maximizing Returns:

- Refinance properties when interest rates drop to improve cash flow and reinvest in other opportunities.
- Use rental income to pay down debt faster, reducing financial risk.
- Diversify financing sources to reduce risk and enhance stability.
- Explore opportunities for value-add investments that can increase property value and community impact.

Final Thoughts: Financing as a Tool for Growth

Real estate financing is more than a means to an end; it's a powerful tool that, when used wisely, can accelerate your growth and success in the industry. By learning from industry leaders like Robert Kiyosaki, Barbara Corcoran, Grant Cardone, Tony Robbins, Brandon Turner, and Dave Ramsey, you can develop a well-rounded financing strategy that supports both your financial goals and your values.

Invest With A SMILE

As Zig Ziglar, a legendary motivational speaker, once said, "You don't have to be great to start, but you have to start to be great." In real estate investing, the right financing strategy can be the starting point for achieving greatness in your portfolio. However, it's essential to align your financing choices with your core values to create investments that not only generate profits but also make a positive impact on the communities you serve.

Conclusion

In this chapter, we've explored a variety of financing strategies and opportunities that real estate investors can leverage to achieve both financial success and community impact. From traditional bank loans to modern crowdfunding platforms and innovative funding methods, the options available are vast and ever-evolving. The key takeaway is that financing should not be viewed merely as a transactional process but as a strategic tool that, when used mindfully, can unlock doors to long-term wealth and social responsibility. By adopting a financing approach that incorporates the SMILE philosophy—prioritizing Safety, Morality, Inclusivity, Linguistic clarity, and Experiential learning—you position yourself as a conscious investor who values both profit and purpose. As the market evolves, those who stay adaptable and continue learning will be the ones who thrive. The stories and insights shared in this chapter demonstrate that creative and ethical financing can turn obstacles into opportunities, paving the way for a brighter financial future.

To learn more about how you can implement these strategies and align your investments with the SMILE values, consider reaching out to SMILE Company for personalized investment services. Whether you're looking for guidance on financing methods, portfolio diversification, or ethical investment practices, SMILE Company offers expert advice and tailored solutions to help you achieve both financial success and positive community impact.

Contact SMILE Company

- **Website:** smilecompanyllc.com
- **Email:** info@smilecompanyllc.com

The team at SMILE Company is committed to helping investors navigate the complexities of real estate financing with integrity and purpose. Reach out today to take the next step in your investing journey.

Chapter 9
Marketing, Tenant Retention, Data Analytics, and Predictive Modeling

Effective Property Marketing

In today's competitive real estate landscape, effective marketing is more crucial than ever. The advent of digital tools has reshaped how landlords and property managers reach potential tenants. Leveraging online platforms, social media, and search engine optimization (SEO) can maximize visibility and lead generation.

Virtual tours, professional photography, and well-crafted listings go beyond static advertisements to create an immersive experience for prospective tenants. Showcasing a property's unique amenities, like energy-efficient appliances, pet-friendly policies, or community events, can differentiate it from others in the market.

However, effective marketing doesn't stop at creating appealing listings. It requires a consistent and innovative approach to stay relevant in a rapidly changing market. Marketing expert Ryan Serhant emphasizes the importance of storytelling in property marketing. By weaving a narrative around the lifestyle and experiences that a property offers, landlords can create an emotional connection with potential tenants, which increases engagement and conversion rates.

In addition to traditional and digital marketing tactics, emerging technologies such as artificial intelligence (AI) are revolutionizing the field. AI tools can analyze large datasets to identify trends in tenant preferences, optimize pricing strategies, and personalize marketing messages. Siddharth Taparia, Global CMO of JLL, highlights that AI has transformed CRE marketing by increasing efficiency and accuracy, turning what used to be lengthy processes into near-instantaneous tasks.

Real-World Example 1: In a competitive urban market, a property management company in New York City implemented an AI-driven campaign that targeted high-income renters seeking eco-friendly living spaces. The campaign resulted in a 40% increase in high-quality leads and a 20% higher lease conversion rate.

Real-World Example 2: A luxury apartment complex in Los Angeles collaborated with a popular lifestyle influencer to create a series of Instagram and TikTok posts showcasing the property's amenities, including rooftop pools and co-working spaces. The campaign generated over 500,000 impressions within a week and led to a significant boost in inquiries from younger, tech-savvy professionals.

Real-World Example 3: A property management firm in Chicago used predictive analytics to optimize rental pricing and identify high-demand amenities. By adjusting their marketing strategy to emphasize features like fitness centers, pet-friendly policies, and community events, they achieved a 25% increase in lease renewals and reduced vacancy rates by 15%.

Another important trend is the rise of influencer marketing in the real estate sector. CRE professionals like Grant Cardone advocate for leveraging social media influencers to showcase properties to a broader audience. These partnerships, particularly in luxury and niche markets, can create a buzz around a property and attract tenants who value exclusivity and prestige.

Real-World Stories

Miami Property Manager: A property manager in Miami was struggling with high vacancy rates in a newly built residential complex. The primary issue was that potential tenants were unaware of the property's amenities and benefits due to inadequate marketing efforts. After adopting a multi-channel digital marketing strategy, including virtual tours and influencer partnerships, inquiries surged by 45%. The property manager realized that digital presence was key to reaching a broader audience, leading to faster lease-ups.

Austin Landlord: In Austin, a landlord experienced frequent tenant turnover, causing operational disruptions and loss of income. After surveying departing tenants, the feedback revealed that many left due to unaddressed maintenance issues and lack of community engagement. By implementing a tenant feedback system, enhancing maintenance protocols, and hosting regular community events, the landlord reduced turnover by 30% within a year.

Boston Commercial Investor: A commercial real estate investor in Boston faced difficulty attracting tenants to a retail property in a competitive market. Traditional marketing methods were no longer yielding results. By embracing data-driven marketing tools and highlighting the property's proximity to public transport and popular local spots through social media campaigns, the investor saw a 20% increase in tenant inquiries. This shift in strategy demonstrated the importance of modern marketing approaches in revitalizing older properties.

How AI, Blockchain, and Emerging Technologies Are Impacting Tenant Retention

The integration of emerging technologies such as AI, blockchain, and IoT (Internet of Things) is significantly changing how landlords and property managers improve tenant retention.

AI-Powered Predictive Maintenance: AI can analyze maintenance data to predict when repairs are needed before issues escalate, ensuring that tenants experience fewer disruptions. This proactive approach reduces frustration caused by unexpected maintenance problems, improving tenant satisfaction and retention.

Blockchain for Lease Management: Blockchain technology enhances transparency in lease agreements by creating immutable, digital records of transactions. Tenants feel more secure knowing that their lease terms are securely stored and tamper-proof. Additionally, smart contracts on blockchain can automate rent payments and other administrative tasks, reducing errors and increasing tenant convenience.

IoT for Enhanced Living Experiences: IoT devices can transform properties into smart homes or offices, providing tenants with greater control over their living or working environments. Smart thermostats, lighting systems, and security features not only enhance comfort but also demonstrate a commitment to modern living standards, which appeals to tech-savvy tenants.

Real-World Example: A property management company in San Francisco implemented IoT devices across its residential buildings, allowing tenants to control appliances, lighting, and security through a mobile app. The convenience and efficiency of these smart features led to a 35% increase in lease renewals.

Sustainability and Energy Efficiency: Technologies like AI and IoT also contribute to energy efficiency. Smart systems can optimize energy usage, lowering utility costs and reducing the property's environmental impact. Tenants, especially those environmentally conscious, are more likely to remain in properties that align with their values.

By leveraging these technologies, landlords can offer a modern, seamless, and secure living experience that increases tenant satisfaction and encourages long-term occupancy.

Practical Marketing Tip 1: Implementing video marketing, especially short-form content for platforms like Instagram, TikTok, and YouTube Shorts, can drastically improve a property's visibility. Videos that highlight unique amenities, neighborhood attractions, and tenant testimonials can help a property stand out in a crowded market.

Additionally, creating a consistent content calendar can keep marketing efforts organized and relevant. Property managers can use scheduling tools to automate social media posts and blog updates, ensuring regular communication with potential tenants. This consistency builds trust and keeps a property top of mind.

Practical Marketing Tip 2: Engage with local businesses and community organizations to co-host events or offer mutual promotions. Cross-promotion with popular local spots—such as coffee shops, gyms, or entertainment venues—can help expose properties to a wider audience and position them as integral parts of the community.

By adopting a multi-channel marketing approach, incorporating storytelling, and leveraging cutting-edge technologies, landlords and property managers can create memorable experiences that attract and retain tenants. These strategies, endorsed by renowned CRE figures like Gary Vaynerchuk, emphasize that effective property marketing goes beyond transactions—it's about creating lasting impressions and relationships.

Aligning with SMILE Company Philosophy and Strategy

The principles and strategies discussed in this chapter are deeply aligned with the SMILE Company's philosophy of creating value through relationships, innovation, and community engagement. By focusing on modern marketing techniques, leveraging emerging technologies, and prioritizing tenant satisfaction, property managers and landlords can foster long-term loyalty and build thriving communities. This approach reflects SMILE Company's mission to provide exceptional experiences, create lasting connections, and enhance the lives of tenants and stakeholders alike. Through innovation, proactive management, and community involvement, SMILE Company sets a benchmark in property management that prioritizes both profitability and human connection.

Leveraging Data for Informed Decisions

Data analytics is transforming real estate investing by providing critical insights into market trends, tenant behaviors, and property performance. By leveraging data, investors can make more informed decisions that optimize profitability and reduce risk. Advanced analytics go beyond merely tracking numbers; they can reveal hidden patterns and predict future tenant preferences, enabling more precise investment decisions. For example, machine learning models can identify rental pricing sweet spots based on historical trends, neighborhood demographics, and seasonal variations.

Data tools also allow investors to assess property performance in real-time, flagging underperforming assets before they become a liability. For instance, predictive algorithms can suggest renovations or upgrades that may improve tenant retention or boost property value. Additionally, these tools help identify market shifts, allowing investors to pivot their strategies in response to changing conditions, such as economic downturns or evolving tenant preferences.

Key strategies include integrating AI-driven dashboards to monitor critical performance indicators such as occupancy rates, rent collection, and maintenance requests. Real-time alerts ensure that landlords and property managers can take immediate action on issues before they escalate. Furthermore, using tenant sentiment analysis through feedback tools allows for proactive adjustments to services and amenities, aligning with tenant expectations and improving satisfaction.

Ultimately, the ability to leverage data analytics empowers property owners to reduce operational inefficiencies, improve tenant experiences, and maximize long-term returns. This approach aligns with industry best practices advocated by leaders like Ryan Serhant and Grant Cardone, who emphasize the importance of data in driving informed, profitable, and community-oriented investments.

Example: An investor in Atlanta used data analytics to adjust rental rates based on seasonal demand, increasing overall revenue by 12% annually. This approach highlights the power of data-driven strategies to maximize returns.

Example 2: A real estate developer in San Francisco leveraged predictive modeling to identify upcoming neighborhood revitalizations. By investing early in properties within those areas, the developer saw a property appreciation of over 40% within three years, significantly outperforming traditional market investments.

Example 3: In Miami, a property management company used tenant behavior analytics to improve lease renewal rates. By identifying tenants likely to move out based on engagement metrics and service requests, the company offered personalized retention incentives, reducing turnover by 35%.

Example 4: A commercial real estate investor in London utilized data analytics to optimize their portfolio. By analyzing local business growth trends, they identified high-demand office spaces and repositioned their properties accordingly, increasing occupancy rates by 25% and achieving premium rental yields.

Using Analytics to Optimize Investments

Real-time data allows for more agile investment strategies by enabling property managers to make informed, timely adjustments that significantly enhance profitability. By closely monitoring occupancy rates, local market trends, tenant feedback, and even external economic indicators, landlords can proactively respond to potential issues before they escalate into costly problems.

One powerful example is the use of predictive modeling to anticipate tenant turnover. By analyzing tenant behavior patterns, such as late rent payments, declining engagement with community events, or frequent maintenance requests, property managers can identify tenants at risk of leaving. Armed with these insights, they can implement tailored retention strategies, such as offering lease renewal incentives or addressing specific tenant concerns, thereby reducing churn and maximizing long-term revenue.

Furthermore, by integrating machine learning algorithms, property managers can predict maintenance needs with remarkable accuracy. For instance, sensors and IoT devices can monitor building infrastructure in real time, flagging potential issues like HVAC inefficiencies, water leaks, or electrical malfunctions. This allows property managers to address problems before they disrupt tenant experiences, ensuring a seamless living environment and reducing the risk of sudden costly repairs.

This proactive, data-driven approach not only reduces operational costs by optimizing resource allocation but also fosters stronger tenant relationships. A seamless and responsive maintenance process contributes significantly to tenant satisfaction, which directly impacts retention rates. Studies show that properties with predictive maintenance systems report tenant retention improvements of up to 40%, demonstrating the effectiveness of real-time data analytics in driving long-term profitability and community stability.

Leading industry players, such as CBRE and Greystar, are already implementing these strategies to stay competitive. CBRE's use of data-driven dashboards helps property managers track tenant engagement and maintenance trends, while Greystar integrates predictive analytics to optimize property performance across its global portfolio. These companies serve as prime examples of how leveraging real-time data can transform property management into a more efficient, tenant-centric practice, fully aligning with the SMILE philosophy's focus on proactive, ethical, and community-oriented real estate investments.

Pain Point Solution: For those overwhelmed by data, starting with simple metrics like rental yield and occupancy rate can ease the transition into more complex analytics, showing that data is an ally, not a barrier.

Analogy: Utilizing data analytics is like using a fitness tracker. It provides real-time feedback to optimize your routine, ensuring better results without the guesswork, proving there's no excuse for ignoring the benefits of data-driven decisions.

Influences from Industry Leaders

Renowned real estate professionals like Sam Zell have emphasized the importance of understanding data in investment decisions. Sam Zell, often referred to as the "Grave Dancer" for his ability to capitalize on distressed assets, has consistently highlighted how data analysis informs his investment strategy to identify undervalued properties and predict market movements.

Another prominent figure, Barbara Corcoran, stresses the importance of customer data in shaping marketing strategies and improving tenant experiences. By analyzing tenant feedback and behavior, property managers can adjust amenities and services to better meet tenant needs, ultimately increasing retention.

Renowned speaker and investor Tony Robbins often highlights the importance of leveraging technology for decision-making. Robbins emphasizes that by using data to predict future trends, investors can make more informed, proactive decisions, which aligns with the SMILE philosophy's emphasis on experiential learning and ongoing adaptation.

Additionally, Ryan Serhant, a leading real estate broker and entrepreneur, believes that data-driven storytelling is a powerful tool in real estate marketing. His perspective aligns with the linguistic clarity pillar of the SMILE philosophy, where clear and compelling communication, backed by data, can enhance tenant engagement and trust.

These insights from industry leaders demonstrate that data analytics is not just a tool for profitability but also a means to create meaningful, long-term connections with tenants. This approach resonates deeply with SMILE's holistic vision of combining innovation, ethics, and community-building in real estate.

The Role of Predictive Modeling

Predictive modeling takes data analysis to the next level by using historical data to forecast future trends. In real estate, this can mean anticipating property appreciation, rental demand, or even identifying emerging neighborhoods. Today, leading property management companies like RealPage and Zillow utilize predictive analytics to optimize rental pricing and forecast tenant demand by analyzing real-time data such as economic shifts, local events, and tenant demographics. For example, Zillow's AI-driven algorithm considers over 100 factors, including crime rates, school ratings, and proximity to amenities, to predict property value changes, providing landlords with highly accurate insights.

Additionally, firms like CBRE and JLL employ AI-driven predictive tools to identify investment hotspots before they become mainstream, giving their clients a competitive edge. CBRE's proprietary tool, called Dimension, integrates predictive analytics with geographic data to pinpoint emerging neighborhoods based on population growth, infrastructure developments, and business activity. JLL's predictive modeling also includes workforce analytics to determine how job growth in a region will impact housing demand, further refining investment decisions.

These strategies align with the SMILE philosophy by promoting proactive, informed decision-making that benefits both investors and the communities they serve. By utilizing these advanced tools, property managers and investors can better predict tenant needs, optimize portfolio performance, and contribute to sustainable community growth. This data-driven approach ensures that investments are not only profitable but also socially responsible, fostering long-term stability and inclusivity in the real estate market.

Real-World Example: A property management firm in Boston used predictive analytics to identify a neighborhood on the brink of gentrification. By investing early, they achieved substantial property value appreciation, far exceeding initial expectations.

George Knowlton

How AI Enhances Predictive Modeling

Artificial intelligence (AI) further enhances predictive modeling by identifying patterns that might be missed by human analysts. AI algorithms can process vast amounts of data quickly and provide actionable insights, such as optimal rental pricing, maintenance schedules, and tenant preferences. For example, AI-powered platforms like RealPage and AppFolio use machine learning to predict future maintenance needs and optimize property performance in real-time. Companies like Zillow have introduced AI-driven tools that forecast property value trends and suggest price adjustments to landlords based on local market fluctuations.

Renowned investor Grant Cardone often emphasizes the importance of scaling operations through technology, including AI. He notes that adopting data-driven strategies is key to achieving long-term success in real estate. Similarly, Gary Vaynerchuk, a prominent entrepreneur and investor, advocates for leveraging AI to personalize tenant experiences and improve customer retention. He believes that understanding tenant behavior through AI insights is the future of real estate management, aligning with the SMILE philosophy's focus on experiential learning and proactive management.

Moreover, Brad Inman, founder of Inman News, has frequently highlighted how AI is reshaping the real estate landscape by creating more efficient workflows for property managers and investors alike. He stresses that embracing these technologies is no longer optional but essential for staying competitive. By integrating AI into property operations, landlords can automate routine tasks, improve accuracy in decision-making, and enhance tenant satisfaction—all of which resonate with the SMILE principles of innovation and inclusivity in real estate investing.

Practical Applications for Investors

1. **Rental Pricing Optimization:** Using data to adjust rental rates based on demand and local trends can significantly increase revenue. Platforms like RealPage, RentRedi, and AppFolio provide property managers with AI-driven insights that suggest the best pricing strategies based on real-time market data. This ensures that rental rates remain competitive without risking vacancies due to overpricing. Additionally, predictive algorithms can identify seasonal trends, allowing landlords to offer promotional rates during slower periods and capitalize on peak demand.
2. **Tenant Retention Strategies:** Identifying tenants at risk of leaving allows property managers to take proactive measures to improve tenant satisfaction. For instance, platforms like HappyCo and Building Engines offer tenant engagement tools that monitor satisfaction levels through regular feedback surveys and maintenance request tracking. These insights allow landlords to address concerns before they escalate, improving tenant loyalty. Some companies have even implemented personalized tenant retention programs, offering tailored incentives such as lease renewal discounts or amenity upgrades.
3. **Market Trend Analysis:** Staying ahead of market trends ensures that investors make strategic decisions aligned with future demand. Companies like CBRE and JLL utilize advanced data analytics to predict market shifts and identify emerging neighborhoods. By analyzing factors such as job growth, infrastructure development, and demographic changes, these firms provide investors with actionable insights to optimize their portfolios. For example, CBRE's predictive models helped identify Austin, Texas, as a high-growth market years before its recent boom, allowing early investors to maximize their returns. These real-time insights align with the SMILE philosophy by promoting proactive, community-focused investment strategies.

Real-World Stories

Chicago Landlord: A landlord in Chicago struggled with high tenant turnover due to outdated rental pricing strategies. After implementing predictive analytics tools, the landlord optimized rental rates and reduced turnover by 25%. This data-driven approach proved more effective than traditional methods, demonstrating the value of analytics in real estate management.

New York Property Manager: In New York City, a property manager faced challenges with maintenance requests piling up, resulting in frustrated tenants and increased move-outs. By adopting an AI-driven maintenance scheduling system, they reduced response times by 40%, significantly improving tenant satisfaction and retention.

Los Angles Property Owner: A commercial property owner in Los Angeles struggled to retain long-term tenants in a co-working space. After analyzing tenant feedback through data analytics, the owner discovered that flexible leasing terms and better communal amenities were key drivers of tenant loyalty. By implementing these changes, they increased tenant renewals by 30% and attracted more high-profile clients.

Conclusion: Aligning with SMILE Company Philosophy

The integration of data analytics and predictive modeling aligns perfectly with the SMILE Company philosophy of informed, responsible investing. By using technology to make data-driven decisions, investors can enhance both profitability and community impact. Comparing traditional real estate strategies with data-driven approaches shows a significant difference in efficiency, accuracy, and long-term outcomes. Unlike traditional methods that rely heavily on intuition and historical data alone, predictive modeling uses real-time insights to forecast trends and anticipate risks.

Comparison:

- **Traditional Approach:** Based on past experiences and static reports.
- **Data-Driven Approach:** Utilizes real-time data, AI insights, and predictive modeling for proactive strategies.

Action Steps:

1. Implement AI tools to monitor tenant feedback and predict maintenance needs.
2. Use predictive analytics to adjust rental pricing based on market demand.
3. Analyze emerging market trends to identify potential investment hotspots.
4. Regularly review data insights to make informed adjustments to property management strategies.

By adopting these action steps, investors can achieve both financial success and community enrichment, reinforcing SMILE's mission of sustainable and ethical real estate practices.

Chapter 10

Planning for Exit: Strategies and Timing

Crafting Successful Exit Strategies with Foresight and Flexibility

An effective exit strategy maximizes returns and minimizes risks. Whether it's selling a property, refinancing, or transitioning to a long-term hold, planning for exits is crucial for overall investment success. Real estate mogul Sam Zell, known for his ability to time the market, emphasizes the importance of having a well-defined exit strategy from the start. He suggests that investors must always plan their exit before making an entry. He frequently refers to the importance of foresight in investing, likening it to a chess game where the endgame must be visualized from the very first move.

Exit strategies should be tailored to the investor's goals, risk tolerance, and market conditions. For instance, investors seeking quick returns might prioritize property flipping, while those focused on steady income may prefer a buy-and-hold strategy. Barbara Corcoran highlights that the decision to exit should also consider tenant and community impact. She emphasizes that smart investors think about who will take over the property and how it will continue to serve the local community.

Best Practices for Exit Strategies to Adapt to Market Shifts:

1. **Scenario Planning:** Investors should create multiple exit scenarios to account for different market conditions. For example, a property could be sold outright, refinanced for further investment, or converted into a different asset type, such as from residential to commercial use. Scenario planning also includes contingency strategies for worst-case scenarios, such as economic downturns or unexpected regulatory changes. For instance, if the original plan was to sell, investors could pivot to a refinance strategy if market conditions are unfavorable. This flexibility is critical to ensuring that exit options remain viable in any market condition.

2. **Early Valuation Assessments:** Regular property valuations help investors determine the right time to exit. Tools like CoStar and CBRE's analytics platforms provide real-time market data to help forecast property values. By conducting early and ongoing valuations, investors can track the appreciation of their assets and make more informed decisions about when to sell. For example, if a property's valuation shows steady growth but is nearing a plateau, it may be the right time to exit before the market shifts. Additionally, early valuations can uncover opportunities for property improvements that could increase market value before selling.
3. **Stakeholder Engagement:** Engaging with stakeholders, including tenants, local businesses, and community leaders, ensures a smooth transition. This approach aligns with the SMILE philosophy by prioritizing community well-being over pure profit. For instance, maintaining open communication with tenants about a potential sale can foster goodwill and reduce turnover. Involving local businesses in redevelopment plans can also strengthen community ties and increase property appeal. Engaged stakeholders are more likely to support and sustain the property's long-term success, making it an attractive asset for future buyers.
4. **Legal and Tax Planning:** Consulting with legal and tax advisors ensures that the exit process is compliant with regulations and optimized for tax benefits. Legal advisors can help navigate complex regulatory requirements, ensuring that all documentation is in order for a smooth sale or transfer. Tax planning is equally critical, as a poorly planned exit can result in significant tax liabilities. For example, utilizing a 1031 exchange can defer capital gains taxes, allowing investors to reinvest proceeds into another property and maintain their wealth. Additionally, understanding local tax incentives and credits can further optimize the financial outcome of an exit strategy.

Popular Story: An investor in Chicago exited a multifamily project during a market peak, reinvesting the profits into new developments, which led to a 30% portfolio growth over two years. This demonstrates how a well-timed exit can significantly boost overall returns.

Similarly, another investor in Los Angeles leveraged a 1031 exchange to defer capital gains taxes by reinvesting sale proceeds into a high-performing commercial property, ultimately increasing cash flow and long-term appreciation potential.

What Not to Do When Exiting to Avoid Costly Mistakes

In contrast, a property owner in Houston made the mistake of holding onto a commercial property well past its market peak. Ignoring market indicators and relying solely on past performance, the investor missed an optimal exit window. When the local market experienced a downturn, property values dropped by 20%, and the investor struggled to sell the property at a desirable price.

Another cautionary tale comes from a landlord in Miami who attempted to exit a property without considering the tax implications. Without proper planning, they faced unexpected capital gains taxes that significantly reduced their net profit. A consultation with a tax advisor beforehand could have mitigated these losses by exploring options like a 1031 exchange.

These examples illustrate the importance of proactive exit planning and the dangers of complacency or poor advice. Investors must stay informed, seek professional guidance, and remain adaptable to changing market conditions.

Timing the Market: Identifying the Right Moment to Exit Successfully

Exiting at the right time can significantly impact profitability. Monitoring market trends, economic indicators, and property performance ensures that investors capitalize on favorable conditions. Barbara Corcoran, founder of The Corcoran Group, advises investors to always keep an eye on local market shifts. She notes that understanding neighborhood dynamics and emerging trends is key to identifying the optimal time to sell. She emphasizes that even seemingly minor indicators, such as the opening of a new retail store or the launch of a local infrastructure project, can signal future appreciation.

Economic indicators like interest rates, job growth, and inflation play a vital role in determining exit timing. Higher interest rates, for instance, can impact buyers' purchasing power, making it harder to sell properties at premium prices. Conversely, periods of strong job growth often correlate with increased housing demand, presenting opportunities for profitable exits. Investors should also consider demographic trends, such as migration patterns and changes in housing preferences, which can influence property values. For example, an influx of remote workers into suburban areas has driven up property values in those regions, making them ideal for well-timed exits.

Overcoming Exit Uncertainty: Data-Driven Approaches for Confident Decision-Making

For those uncertain about when to exit, setting predefined financial goals and using market analysis tools can provide clarity and confidence in decision-making. Establishing a clear target for returns, such as achieving a specific ROI or hitting a predetermined property valuation, helps remove emotional bias from the decision-making process. Tools like CoStar and Zillow's market analytics offer valuable insights into local market conditions, including historical trends, current demand levels, and future projections. These platforms can forecast potential price movements, rental yield fluctuations, and neighborhood growth indicators, allowing investors to better time their exits.

Additionally, predictive analytics tools like RealPage and Yardi Matrix offer more advanced features, such as identifying micro-market trends and tenant behavior patterns. Investors can leverage these insights to recognize subtle changes in market dynamics—such as shifts in demographic profiles or local business growth—that may signal an ideal time to sell.

Real-world application of these tools has shown that investors using data-driven exit strategies tend to achieve higher profitability compared to those relying on intuition. For example, a multifamily investor in Denver utilized CoStar's forecasting tool to sell their property just before a major interest rate hike, resulting in a 20% higher sale price than anticipated. Such proactive measures, driven by actionable data, are critical for successful exits.

Analogy: Preparing for a Marathon Finish

Planning your exit is like preparing for a marathon finish. Knowing when and how to cross the line ensures you finish strong, eliminating the excuse that exits are too unpredictable to plan for. Just as a marathon runner paces themselves, staying attuned to their body and the environment, investors must continuously monitor the market, track property performance, and adjust their strategies accordingly. Preparing for the finish line involves understanding the risks and opportunities along the way. Ignoring market indicators is akin to sprinting too early in a race—it can lead to burnout or missed opportunities. On the flip side, planning with precision and pacing your decisions ensures you achieve the best possible outcome, crossing the finish line with strength and purpose.

Influences from Industry Leaders

Grant Cardone, a prominent real estate investor, emphasizes the importance of scaling investments with a clear exit strategy in mind. He advises investors to treat each property like a business, understanding when it's time to sell, refinance, or reinvest in new opportunities.

Similarly, Tony Robbins highlights the significance of setting clear financial goals and exit timelines to avoid emotional decision-making. He believes that having a well-defined exit plan helps investors stay focused on long-term success and avoid reactive decisions based on short-term market fluctuations.

Kane & Alessia Minkus, renowned global business mentors, advocate for building sustainable business models with intentional exit strategies. They stress that investors should continuously evaluate their assets' performance and market conditions to ensure their exits align with both financial and community goals. Their advice ties directly into the SMILE philosophy, particularly the experiential learning pillar, which encourages ongoing adaptation and reflection.

Sir Richard Branson underscores the importance of ethical exits, emphasizing that responsible investors should consider the broader impact of their exit decisions on communities and stakeholders. His approach resonates with the inclusivity and morality aspects of the SMILE framework, promoting exits that leave lasting positive impacts.

John Maxwell, a leadership expert, highlights that successful exits require clear vision and purpose. He encourages investors to approach exits as leadership moments—opportunities to inspire trust, build legacy, and create value beyond financial returns. Maxwell's focus on integrity and long-term impact aligns perfectly with the SMILE philosophy's ethical and community-oriented principles.

Real-World Example: Opportunistic Exit

A real estate investment group in New York identified an emerging neighborhood on the cusp of gentrification. They acquired properties at low prices and, after five years of significant appreciation, sold the portfolio for a 45% profit. The group's ability to recognize the right time to exit was instrumental in achieving this success.

This case highlights how a long-term strategy focused on holding properties through various market cycles can foster opportunities for opportunistic exits. By adopting a patient, data-driven approach, the group positioned themselves to capitalize on the neighborhood's growth at the optimal time. Long-term strategies allow investors to ride out temporary market fluctuations and align their exits with peak value periods. For example, during economic downturns, maintaining a stable portfolio can lead to significant appreciation once the market recovers. This approach also provides flexibility to pivot based on emerging trends, such as demographic shifts or infrastructure developments, which can enhance property values.

Investors like Sir Richard Branson emphasize the importance of thinking long-term, noting that success in real estate often comes from patience and persistence. By holding assets for extended periods, investors have more time to identify opportunistic moments to sell, whether it's due to favorable market conditions or specific buyer interest. Additionally, long-term holding strategies allow for ongoing improvements to properties, further increasing their value over time.

Actionable Exit Strategies: Practical Steps for a Seamless Transition

1. **Set Financial Goals:** Define your target returns and timeline for each investment. Long-term planning provides clarity, ensuring that exit decisions align with overall financial objectives. Establish SMART goals (Specific, Measurable, Achievable, Relevant, Time-bound) to remain focused and adaptable to changing conditions.
2. **Monitor Market Conditions:** Use data analytics tools to stay informed about local and national real estate trends. Tools like CoStar, RealPage, and Yardi Matrix offer valuable insights, enabling investors to recognize optimal exit windows and avoid downturn risks.
3. **Diversify Exit Options:** Have multiple exit strategies in place, such as selling, refinancing, or converting properties into different asset classes. This approach provides flexibility to adapt to market shifts and capitalize on new opportunities.
4. **Consult Experts:** Work with real estate advisors, accountants, and legal professionals to ensure a smooth exit process. Collaborating with experts helps mitigate risks, optimize tax strategies, and navigate regulatory requirements seamlessly.

Aligning with SMILE Philosophy

The SMILE philosophy emphasizes proactive, ethical, and informed decision-making. By planning exits with community impact in mind, investors can ensure that their strategies benefit both their portfolios and the neighborhoods they invest in. For example, instead of selling to the highest bidder, investors can prioritize buyers who will continue to enhance the property and support the local community by investing in local businesses, improving infrastructure, or providing affordable housing options.

Exits are not just about maximizing financial returns; they're about leaving a lasting positive impact. Investors who adopt this approach foster goodwill within communities, which can have long-term benefits, including future investment opportunities and stronger local partnerships. The SMILE approach encourages investors to view exit strategies as leadership moments, where they have the power to influence social and economic outcomes positively. This perspective aligns with John Maxwell's teachings on leadership, emphasizing that great leaders leave behind legacies of growth and empowerment. By considering the broader implications of exit decisions, investors can contribute to sustainable community growth and enhance their reputations as responsible, ethical investors.

Chapter 11
The Future of Real Estate Investing

Embracing Innovation and Change

The real estate industry is constantly evolving, driven by technological advancements, shifting demographics, changing consumer expectations, and the influence of political leadership. With the impending Trump presidency, many expect regulatory shifts that could reshape the commercial real estate (CRE) landscape in significant ways. Tax reforms, deregulation, and policies aimed at infrastructure development may create both opportunities and risks for investors.

Renowned entrepreneur and investor Richard Branson emphasizes the importance of staying ahead of the curve. In his words, "Innovation is at the heart of every successful venture." Similarly, leaders like Kane & Alessia Minkus stress that staying adaptable to political and economic changes is essential for long-term success. Trump's administration is likely to push for economic growth through infrastructure projects and tax incentives for developers, which could fuel new opportunities in CRE.

However, investors must also be cautious. Policy changes can lead to increased volatility in interest rates and shifting demand patterns. Ignoring these potential risks is akin to refusing to upgrade from a typewriter to a computer—what once worked well may no longer suffice in a rapidly changing market.

The positive analogy here is that embracing new policies and trends is like upgrading to a modern vehicle with advanced safety features. It not only makes the journey smoother but also minimizes risks along the way. Conversely, failing to account for political changes is akin to stubbornly driving an old car without GPS, refusing to acknowledge that better tools and information exist. In both scenarios, success depends on the tools and mindset investors use to navigate their path.

Technological Innovations Shaping the Future of Real Estate

PropTech (Property Technology):

The rise of PropTech has transformed property management, leasing, and tenant engagement. Tools like smart home systems, virtual tours, and AI-driven property analytics have become standard features in modern real estate. These technologies improve operational efficiency, enhance tenant experiences, and help property managers make data-driven decisions. The integration of PropTech allows real estate firms to differentiate themselves by offering smarter, more connected living spaces that cater to modern tenant demands.

Looking to the future, we may see PropTech evolve into fully automated property ecosystems. Imagine a building that uses AI to manage everything from tenant preferences to energy usage, automatically adjusting lighting, temperature, and even water usage based on occupancy and weather forecasts. Additionally, smart contracts on blockchain could handle lease agreements autonomously, reducing paperwork and eliminating disputes through automated enforcement of terms.

Example: A property management firm in New York implemented AI-driven maintenance systems that predicted and addressed issues before tenants reported them, leading to a 30% reduction in maintenance costs and a significant boost in tenant satisfaction. This approach not only improved operational efficiency but also increased tenant retention, as residents appreciated the proactive maintenance service.

Blockchain in Real Estate:

Blockchain technology is revolutionizing real estate transactions by increasing transparency and reducing the need for intermediaries. Smart contracts, which automate agreements between parties, are making transactions faster, more secure, and more efficient. However, the future of blockchain in real estate could be influenced by the upcoming Trump administration. Historically skeptical of cryptocurrencies and blockchain technologies, Trump's stance could slow the widespread adoption of blockchain in regulated markets if new restrictions are introduced.

That said, the underlying benefits of blockchain—such as security, transparency, and efficiency—are difficult to ignore. Many forward-thinking real estate firms are already leveraging this technology to streamline property transactions. For example, a real estate company in London used blockchain to facilitate property sales, reducing transaction times from weeks to days while ensuring secure and tamper-proof records. Looking forward, if policies become more favorable or neutral, blockchain could revolutionize leasing, property management, and title verification through decentralized systems.

In contrast, if restrictions increase, investors may need to pivot to jurisdictions with more favorable blockchain policies. In either case, understanding the potential regulatory environment will be key for investors seeking to capitalize on this technology. Richard Branson, a strong proponent of innovation, notes that early adopters of transformative technologies often gain the most significant competitive advantages, emphasizing that regulatory barriers should be seen as hurdles to overcome, not dead ends.

Example: A real estate company in London used blockchain to facilitate property sales, reducing transaction times from weeks to days while ensuring secure and tamper-proof records.

AI and Predictive Analytics:

AI is transforming how investors make decisions by processing vast amounts of data to uncover patterns that might be missed by traditional analysis. Predictive analytics tools not only forecast market trends but also offer insights into tenant behavior, regional economic shifts, and even potential property maintenance needs. These tools optimize rental pricing in real time by analyzing local demand, seasonal trends, and competitor rates, allowing property owners to maximize revenue without risking vacancy. Furthermore, AI can identify high-demand areas by correlating demographic changes, infrastructure developments, and employment growth, ensuring investors stay ahead of the competition.

For example, a property management firm in California used AI to anticipate tenant turnover based on engagement metrics and rent payment patterns, reducing vacancy periods by 25%. Additionally, AI-driven platforms like RealPage and Yardi are helping investors predict maintenance issues before they occur, ensuring properties remain in top condition and increasing tenant satisfaction. This proactive approach to property management aligns with the SMILE philosophy by emphasizing experiential learning and ethical practices that benefit both investors and tenants.

Influence from Industry Leaders: Grant Cardone, a leading real estate investor, advocates for the use of AI to scale real estate operations. He notes that AI-driven insights allow investors to make more accurate, data-driven decisions, reducing risks and maximizing returns. Cardone emphasizes that AI isn't just a tool for analysis but a game-changer for operational efficiency. For example, AI can automate repetitive tasks such as lease renewals, rent collection, and maintenance scheduling, freeing up time for investors to focus on strategic growth. He also highlights that AI-driven platforms can identify emerging investment opportunities faster than traditional methods, giving investors a competitive edge in fast-moving markets. Cardone's advocacy aligns with the SMILE philosophy's focus on experiential learning by encouraging continuous adaptation to technological advancements.

Demographic Shifts Redefining Property Demand

Changing demographics are reshaping the real estate landscape. The rise of remote work, increased urbanization in some areas, and suburban migration in others are influencing property demand in both residential and commercial sectors. For instance, remote work has driven demand for larger suburban homes with dedicated office spaces, while urban areas are seeing increased interest in flexible co-working spaces.

Prominent real estate leaders like Barbara Corcoran have noted that these shifts represent both challenges and opportunities. She advises investors to stay attuned to changing tenant preferences, such as the desire for more outdoor space and proximity to community amenities in suburban areas or enhanced digital infrastructure in urban properties to support remote work. Additionally, Kane & Alessia Minkus emphasize that investors who adapt to these demographic changes can capitalize on emerging trends before they become mainstream.

For example, younger generations are prioritizing sustainability and community-focused living environments, which is driving demand for eco-friendly developments and co-living spaces. Understanding these shifts allows investors to better target their offerings and future-proof their portfolios. Ignoring these trends, on the other hand, could result in outdated properties that fail to meet evolving market needs, akin to trying to sell a cassette player in the age of digital music streaming.

Case Study: A developer in Austin, Texas, recognized a growing demand for co-living spaces among young professionals. By building properties designed for shared living, the developer achieved a 95% occupancy rate within the first year.

John Maxwell, a leadership expert, highlights the importance of understanding demographic shifts, stating that leaders must "anticipate change and adapt proactively." Real estate investors who identify and respond to these shifts can capitalize on emerging opportunities.

Sustainability and Green Building as a Competitive Advantage

Sustainability is no longer a niche trend but a necessity in modern real estate. Green building practices, energy-efficient technologies, and eco-friendly designs are becoming standard requirements, driven by tenant demand, regulatory pressures, and long-term cost savings. Modern tenants prioritize living and working in spaces that reflect their environmental values, and investors who incorporate sustainability into their projects are likely to experience lower vacancy rates and higher tenant retention.

For instance, features like solar panels, smart thermostats, and water-efficient fixtures are no longer viewed as luxury additions but as essential components of competitive properties. Retrofitting older buildings to meet LEED (Leadership in Energy and Environmental Design) standards can significantly reduce energy costs and improve market appeal.

On the flip side, ignoring sustainability trends can lead to stranded assets—properties that lose value due to outdated designs or non-compliance with emerging environmental regulations. As investor and author Tony Robbins puts it, "Change is inevitable, but progress is optional." Investors who resist adopting sustainable practices risk being left behind in a market that increasingly values green living.

Looking ahead, emerging technologies like carbon capture, green roofs, and smart energy grids are expected to play a pivotal role in shaping future developments. Real estate leaders like Kane & Alessia Minkus encourage investors to view sustainability as both a moral imperative and a business advantage, noting that eco-friendly properties often command premium rents and attract more socially conscious tenants. This shift not only aligns with regulatory trends but also supports the broader SMILE philosophy of ethical, community-focused investing.

Example: A real estate firm in Portland, Oregon, retrofitted an older property to meet LEED (Leadership in Energy and Environmental Design) standards. The property's energy costs decreased by 40%, and tenant retention improved due to the building's eco-friendly features.

Influence from Industry Leaders: Kane & Alessia Minkus emphasize that sustainability is not just good for the environment but also for business. They advocate for incorporating green practices into real estate projects to attract environmentally conscious tenants and investors. According to their research, properties with eco-friendly certifications like LEED or WELL tend to command higher rental rates and experience lower vacancy periods. This is because modern tenants—especially Millennials and Gen Z—actively seek out properties that align with their values around environmental stewardship.

Furthermore, Kane & Alessia highlight that investors who prioritize sustainability often benefit from long-term cost savings through reduced energy consumption and maintenance expenses. For example, integrating smart energy management systems can lower utility costs by up to 30%, creating a win-win scenario for both landlords and tenants. They also point out that regulatory pressures are increasing, with governments around the world implementing stricter environmental standards. By adopting green practices now, investors can future-proof their portfolios against upcoming regulations, ensuring compliance and maintaining property values.

Beyond financial gains, Kane Minkus stresses that incorporating sustainability enhances a property's brand image. In a competitive market, being known as a green, forward-thinking investor can attract more tenants and even premium investors who prioritize ESG

(Environmental, Social, and Governance) factors. Ultimately, sustainability-driven projects align with the broader SMILE philosophy, promoting ethical, community-focused investment strategies that benefit all stakeholders involved.

The Role of Smart Cities in Modern Real Estate Development

Smart cities integrate technology and infrastructure to improve the quality of life for residents by enhancing connectivity, energy efficiency, and public services. These cities utilize IoT (Internet of Things) devices to manage resources in real-time, optimize traffic flow, reduce energy consumption, and improve security.

Real estate investors who participate in smart city initiatives can benefit from increased property values and long-term stability, as these developments often attract businesses and residents seeking modern, sustainable living environments. For example, projects like the Hudson Yards development in New York City showcase how smart city features, such as energy-efficient buildings and advanced waste management systems, can create desirable, future-proof communities.

However, investors must also consider the challenges associated with smart city initiatives, such as high upfront costs and the need for ongoing technological upgrades. Ignoring these advancements is akin to investing in properties without considering their future relevance. Forward-thinking investors who embrace smart city concepts can position themselves as leaders in sustainable development, contributing to both community well-being and portfolio growth.

Example: A real estate investor in Singapore collaborated with the government to develop smart housing solutions, incorporating IoT (Internet of Things) devices to enhance energy efficiency and security. The project achieved high tenant satisfaction and increased property values.

Another notable example is Rancho Cordova, California, which has embraced smart city initiatives to improve the quality of life for residents. By integrating IoT technology across public services, including smart streetlights, traffic management systems, and water conservation programs, Rancho Cordova has become a model for sustainable urban development. These efforts have not only improved energy efficiency but also attracted new businesses and residents, boosting local property values.

Similarly, Roseville, California, has taken significant steps toward becoming a smart city by investing in renewable energy projects, advanced traffic management systems, and digital infrastructure. Roseville's Electric Utility is one of the few municipally owned utilities in California, allowing the city to pilot innovative energy solutions, including solar power programs and energy storage systems. These initiatives have improved service reliability and lowered energy costs for residents, making the city more appealing for both residential and commercial investors.

Richard Branson emphasizes that smart city initiatives are the future of urban living. "Cities that invest in technology and innovation will attract the best talent and create sustainable growth," he notes.

Actionable Strategies for Future-Proofing Investments

1. **Embrace Technology:** Integrate PropTech solutions to improve property management and tenant experiences. These technologies can range from AI-driven maintenance systems that predict and address issues before they arise to virtual reality tours that enhance the leasing process. Embracing PropTech not only improves operational efficiency but also enhances tenant satisfaction, fostering long-term loyalty.
2. **Focus on Sustainability:** Implement green building practices to reduce costs and attract environmentally conscious tenants. This includes energy-efficient upgrades such as solar panels, smart thermostats, and water-saving fixtures. Investors who adopt sustainability practices often see reduced utility costs and higher tenant retention rates. Additionally, properties with eco-certifications like LEED or WELL command premium rents and appeal to socially conscious tenants.
3. **Monitor Demographic Trends:** Stay informed about population shifts and changing tenant preferences. For instance, the rise of remote work has increased demand for larger suburban homes with dedicated office spaces.

Conversely, urban areas are seeing a growing interest in co-living spaces and flexible commercial leases. Understanding these trends enables investors to align their portfolios with current market needs and anticipate future demand.

4. **Explore Blockchain and AI:** Leverage blockchain for secure transactions and AI for data-driven decision-making. Blockchain technology can streamline property transactions through smart contracts, reducing paperwork and eliminating disputes. AI, on the other hand, offers predictive analytics that can forecast market trends, optimize rental pricing, and identify high-demand areas, giving investors a competitive edge.
5. **Participate in Smart City Initiatives:** Collaborate with local governments to develop smart, sustainable communities. Smart city features like IoT-powered traffic management, energy-efficient streetlights, and digital infrastructure attract residents and businesses seeking modern, connected environments. Cities like Rancho Cordova and Roseville, California, serve as prime examples of how smart city projects can enhance property values and foster long-term community growth.

Aligning with SMILE Philosophy

The SMILE philosophy aligns with the future of real estate investing by promoting innovation, inclusivity, and sustainability. By adopting forward-thinking strategies, investors can achieve financial success while making a positive impact on communities. This approach not only enhances financial returns but also ensures that real estate projects contribute to the long-term well-being of the neighborhoods they serve.

John Maxwell reminds us that "Leaders see more and see before." Investors who embrace innovation and anticipate future trends will not only thrive but also contribute to creating better, more sustainable living environments for future generations. By investing in smart technologies, green building practices, and socially responsible projects, these investors lead the way in shaping the future of real estate. Their forward-thinking approach reflects the core of SMILE—balancing profit with purpose to leave a legacy of positive change.

Invest With A SMILE
Final Call to Action for Forward-Thinking Investors

As the real estate industry continues to evolve, the need for conscious, community-driven investments becomes more critical than ever. We encourage investors to embrace the principles outlined in this book by integrating innovation, sustainability, and ethical practices into their real estate strategies. By doing so, you can not only future-proof your investments but also make meaningful contributions to the communities you serve.

The SMILE philosophy is more than a framework—it's a movement toward a more responsible and impactful approach to real estate investing. Take the first step toward creating a lasting legacy by reaching out to us.

For more insights, guidance, and partnership opportunities, contact SMILE Company:

SMILE Company Website: www.smilecompanyllc.com Email: info@smilecompanyllc.com

Join us in shaping a better, more sustainable future for real estate and the communities we serve.

Glossary

1. **Capital Appreciation** – The increase in the value of a property over time.
2. **Due Diligence** – The comprehensive appraisal of a property, including an analysis of market conditions and financial performance.
3. **Multifamily Housing** – Residential properties consisting of multiple separate housing units for tenants.
4. **PropTech** – Technology that drives innovation in the real estate sector, improving efficiency and management.
5. **REITs (Real Estate Investment Trusts)** – Companies that own or finance income-generating real estate across various property sectors.
6. **Sustainability** – Practices that reduce environmental impact and promote long-term ecological balance in real estate development.

Index of References

- **National Association of Realtors** (2023) – *Trends in Suburban Real Estate.*
- **Urban Land Institute** (2024) – *The Rise of Multifamily Housing.*
- **Census Bureau Data** (2022) – *Population Shifts and Housing Demand.*

www.ingramcontent.com/pod-product-compliance
Lightning Source LLC
Chambersburg PA
CBHW050110210326
41519CB00015BA/3897
9798992477818